CONOR McPHERSON

Conor McPherson was u___ ___ ___
Rum and Vodka (Fly by Night Theatre Co., Dublin); *The Good Thief* (Dublin Theatre Festival; Stewart Parker Award); *This Lime Tree Bower* (Fly by Night Theatre Co. and Bush Theatre, London; Meyer-Whitworth Award); *St Nicholas* (Bush Theatre and Primary Stages, New York); *The Weir* (Royal Court, London, Duke of York's, West End and Walter Kerr Theatre, New York; Laurence Olivier, Evening Standard, Critics' Circle, George Devine Awards); *Dublin Carol* (Royal Court and Atlantic Theater, New York); *Port Authority* (Ambassadors Theatre, West End, Gate Theatre, Dublin and Atlantic Theater, New York); *Shining City* (Royal Court, Gate Theatre, Dublin and Manhattan Theatre Club, New York; Tony Award nomination for Best Play); *The Seafarer* (National Theatre, London, Abbey Theatre, Dublin and Booth Theater, New York; Laurence Olivier, Evening Standard, Tony Award nominations for Best Play); *The Veil* (National Theatre) and *The Night Alive* (Donmar Warehouse, London and Atlantic Theater, New York). Theatre adaptations include Daphne du Maurier's *The Birds* (Gate Theatre, Dublin and Guthrie Theater, Minneapolis), August Strindberg's *The Dance of Death* (Donmar at Trafalgar Studios) and Franz Xaver Kroetz's *The Nest* (Young Vic, London).

Work for the cinema includes *I Went Down*, *Saltwater*, Samuel Beckett's *Endgame*, *The Actors*, *The Eclipse* and *Strangers*. His work for television includes an adaptation of John Banville's *Elegy for April* for the BBC, and the original television drama *Paula* for BBC2.

Awards for his screenwriting include three Best Screenplay Awards from the Irish Film and Television Academy; Spanish Cinema Writers Circle Best Screenplay Award; the CICAE Award for Best Film Berlin Film festival; Jury Prize San Sebastian F   nt Award for
Best Europ

BOB DYLAN

Since bursting into the public's consciousness in the early
1960s, Bob Dylan has sold more than 125 million records, won
eleven Grammy Awards and has six entries in the Grammy Hall
of Fame. His contribution to worldwide culture has been
recognised with many awards, including the 2016 Nobel Prize
for Literature (the first songwriter to receive such a distinction);
America's highest civilian honour, the Presidential Medal of
Freedom, from President Obama in 2012; a Special Citation
Pulitzer Prize in 2008; an Academy Award in 2001 for 'Things
Have Changed' from the film *Wonder Boys*. He released his
thirty-ninth studio album, *Triplicate*, in April 2017, and
continues to tour worldwide.

Conor McPherson

GIRL FROM THE NORTH COUNTRY

Music and Lyrics by
Bob Dylan

NICK HERN BOOKS
London
www.nickhernbooks.co.uk

A Nick Hern Book

Girl from the North Country first published in 2017 by Nick Hern Books Limited, The Glasshouse, 49a Goldhawk Road, London W12 8QP

Introduction copyright © 2017 Conor McPherson
The play *Girl from the North Country* copyright © 2017 Conor McPherson

Copyright information for the individual songs may be found at the back of the book

Conor McPherson has asserted his moral right to be identified as the author of this work

Cover image: © CLIPART OF LLC

Designed and typeset by Nick Hern Books, London
Printed and bound in Great Britain by CPI Group (UK) Ltd

A CIP catalogue record for this book is available from the British Library

ISBN   978 1 84842 655 9

MIX
Paper from
responsible sources
FSC® C020471

Girl from the North Country premiered at The Old Vic, London, on 8 July 2017, with the following cast:

MARIANNE LAINE	Sheila Atim
DR WALKER	Ron Cook
MRS BURKE	Bronagh Gallagher
ELIZABETH LAINE	Shirley Henderson
NICK LAINE	Ciarán Hinds
KATHERINE DRAPER	Claudia Jolly
JOE SCOTT	Arinzé Kene
MRS NEILSEN	Debbie Kurup
ENSEMBLE	Kirsty Malpass
MR PERRY	Jim Norton
ENSEMBLE	Tom Peters
ENSEMBLE	Karl Queensborough
GENE LAINE	Sam Reid
REVEREND MARLOWE	Michael Shaeffer
ELIAS BURKE	Jack Shalloo
MR BURKE	Stanley Townsend

MUSICIANS

Violin & Mandolin	Charlie Brown
Guitars	Pete Callard
Double Bass	Don Richardson

Director	Conor McPherson
Music and Lyrics	Bob Dylan
Designer	Rae Smith
Orchestrator, Arranger and Musical Supervisor	Simon Hale
Lighting Designer	Mark Henderson
Sound Designer	Simon Baker
Musical Director	Alan Berry
Movement Director	Lucy Hind
Casting Director	Jessica Ronane CDG

Introduction

Maybe five years ago I was asked if I might consider writing a
play to feature Bob Dylan's songs. I initially didn't feel this was
something I could do and I had cast it out of my mind when,
one day, walking along, I saw a vision of a guesthouse in
Minnesota in the 1930s.

I had been in Minnesota twice in the years leading up to this –
both times in the dead of winter. The friendliness of the people,
the dry frozen wind, the vast distance from home, these things
had stayed with me. And I saw a way Mr Dylan's songs might
make sense in a play.

I was invited to write down the idea I had seen and send it to
Bob Dylan. A few days later I heard back that Mr Dylan liked
the idea and was happy for me to proceed. Just like that.

And then I received forty albums in the post, covering Mr
Dylan's career. While I owned Dylan albums already, like *Desire*
and *Blood on the Tracks*, and loved many of his songs (often
without knowing he'd written them) performed by hundreds of
artists from The Byrds to Fairport Convention, I had no idea of
the real search he had been on his whole life.

It strikes me that many of Mr Dylan's songs can be sung at any
time, by anyone in any situation, and still make sense and
resonate with that particular place and person and time. When
you realise this you can no longer have any doubt you are in the
presence of a truly great, unique artist.

Working on our production of *Girl from the North Country*,
sometimes I would wake in the night with a Bob Dylan song
going round in my head. The next day I would come into
rehearsals and we'd learn the song and put it in the show. Did it
fit? Did it matter? It always fit somehow.

Many books have been written in an attempt to explore this
universal power. Even though Mr Dylan will say he's often not

sure what his songs mean, he always sings them like he means them. Because he does mean them. Whatever they mean.

Every time I hear these songs I see a picture like I'm watching a movie. Sometimes it's the same, sometimes it's different, but you always see something.

Like Philip Larkin, like James Joyce, Mr Dylan has the rare power of literary compression. Images and conceits are held in unstable relations, forcing an atomic reaction of some kind, creating a new inner world.

But let's talk about his musicality. Spending time with his music has taught me a few things: Firstly, writing something that sounds original is rare, but writing something that sounds original *and* simple at the same time is the mark of genius. Anyone can keep making things more complicated, but to keep a song simple, like it somehow always existed and would have surely been written by someone, someday... try writing that one.

Secondly, Mr Dylan always goes through the right musical door. Listening to a Bob Dylan song is like being in a room you've never been in before. It's full of characters and images and tons of musical atmosphere. But then Bob changes the chords, moving through a bridge or a chorus, and a door opens up in that room, so you go through that door into another room – but it's always the *right* door.

Thirdly, Mr Dylan sings about God a lot. Sometimes God appears as an impossible reflection of yourself. Sometimes as someone you could never know. But however God appears, however Mr Dylan begs for mercy, you understand that cry.

Anyway, I write this on the eve of moving from the rehearsal room to the theatre. Whatever happens next I have no idea. All I can say with any certainty is that having had Mr Dylan's trust to create a piece of work using his songs has been one of the great artistic privileges of my life.

Conor McPherson
London, 2017

For Fionnuala and Sumati

Characters

NICK LAINE, *early fifties, proprietor*
ELIZABETH LAINE, *early fifties, his wife*
MARIANNE LAINE, *nineteen, their daughter*
GENE LAINE, *twenty, their son*
MRS NEILSEN, *early forties, a widow*
MR BURKE, *fifties, erstwhile factory owner*
MRS BURKE, *fifties, his wife*
ELIAS BURKE, *thirty, their son*
JOE SCOTT, *late twenties, a boxer*
REVEREND MARLOWE, *fifties, a Bible salesman*
MR PERRY, *early sixties, a shoe-mender*
DR WALKER, *middle-aged, a physician*
KATHERINE (KATE) DRAPER, *Gene's ex-girlfriend*

Setting

A fair-sized family house, which is now serving as a guesthouse
in Duluth, Minnesota. Winter, 1934.

Note on Lyrics

An ellipsis (…) on its own line indicates an omitted verse or
chorus from within the original song.

*This text went to press before the end of rehearsals and so may
differ slightly from the play as performed.*

ACT ONE

*Actors and musicians on stage to get ready for the live broadcast.
Someone sits a piano and plays and sings. A drummer, double-
bass player and guitar player join in along the way, as do the
cast, harmonizing.*

Sign On The Window

Sign on the window says 'Lonely'
Sign on the door said 'No Company Allowed'
Sign on the street says 'Y' Don't Own Me'
Sign on the porch says 'Three's A Crowd'
Sign on the porch says 'Three's A Crowd'

…

Looks like a-nothing but rain…
Sure gonna be wet tonight on Main Street…
Hope that it don't sleet

*The band take the music down for a few bars while a middle-
aged actor approaches the microphone:*

DR WALKER. Tonight's story begins and ends at a guesthouse
in Duluth, Minnesota, in the winter of 1934. Back here –
some of the guests we'll meet along the way.

*The rising light reveals two figures in the dining room where
there's a table for eating at, some easy chairs near a stove, a
dresser, a piano. ELIZABETH, fifties, sits at the piano picking
out a tune. She has early-onset dementia. Her husband, NICK,
is the same age as ELIZABETH but an agitated energy makes
him seem younger somehow. He puts on an apron and starts
working, setting the table for their guests.*

This is Nick Laine. That's his wife there, Elizabeth. Nick
inherited this house from his granddaddy, but he never had
no head for business. First he lost the stables and stud, then

all the stocks. Managed to remortgage the house long enough for Elizabeth to turn it into decent boarding rooms.

But she hasn't been so good lately. Her dementia crept in so insidiously, so gradually, crueler folk in town said you'd be hard pushed to know the difference. Nick's tryna take care of everything. Trying real hard. Like a man tryna to run through a wall tries real hard.

My name is George Arthur Walker. I'm a doctor. Least I was. Back when this was our world. I healed some bodies in pain. But as we know pain comes in all kinds. Physical, spiritual. Indescribable.

I'll come in the story later, but right now, all you need to know is Nick's made some stew for his family, for the guests. Keep everybody alive another day.

The last verse is sung while NICK *spoons stew in a bowl to cool for* ELIZABETH. *The song finishes out…*

NICK. Elizabeth. (*Pause.*) Elizabeth.

She ignores him.

Elizabeth. Sit down, I'll give you something to eat.

ELIZABETH*'s expression suggests her absence, her presence. She looks at him but otherwise ignores his requests. She goes, bends down under a chair and retrieves a little box. She turns away, hiding it from* NICK. *She opens it, counts through some dollars in there, and closes it again quickly.*

Sit down. Come on. Supper.

Exasperated, he puts her meal down on the table and comes to her, guiding her towards the easy chair near the stove. She resists. This becomes a silent battle of wills as they slowly wrestle. She is surprisingly strong. NICK *gives up, angrily walking away and tossing a plate across the table. She remains standing.*

Alright. Well. Alright.

ELIZABETH. I can hear it.

NICK. What.

ELIZABETH. The girl down the hole.

NICK *looks at her.*

NICK. What?

ELIZABETH. Girl down the hole.

NICK *is startled by someone coming through the kitchen.*

NICK. Hello?

NICK *sees* GENE *in the kitchen.*

Oh.

GENE. Yeah, 'Oh...'

NICK. What are you doing scratching around like that?

GENE. What? I'm hungry!

NICK. You know what time it is? You're only coming in?

GENE. I was working late.

NICK. Working my ass.

GENE. I was working!

NICK. You were drinking.

GENE. You have to drink if you want to sit at the bar.

NICK. Who works in a bar?! You can't work in your room?

GENE. No I can't work in my room.

NICK. Why?

GENE c*omes to the table, putting a book down, picking at bread, while* NICK *continues his work.*

GENE. It's too stultifying.

NICK. Well excuse me! I saw you got a letter. Huh?

GENE. Yeah.

NICK. New York postmark.

GENE. It was nothing.

NICK. Yeah?

GENE. Yeah, nothing, you know.

NICK. You should let me read, you know, some of your stories, some time.

GENE. Yeah?

NICK. Hey I been around.

GENE. Yeah.

NICK. Yeah. I've lived. You can't see it 'cause as far as you're concerned I'm just the old dumb-bell round here. I could read 'em. Tell ya where you might need a little… you know. A little life. A little real life. Maybe we could turn some a those rejection slips into pay cheques, huh?

GENE. Now I know you're desperate.

NICK. Desperate? Well…

GENE. Two minutes ago it wasn't even work, now you wanna do it for me?

NICK. Hey don't ambush me with my own double standards. You don't even know what work is. Get a job, you'll know all about it. What it does to you.

GENE. Get a job where?

NICK (*to himself*). Scribbling in a book isn't work.

GENE. Get a job where?

NICK. Hm?

GENE. Get a job where?

NICK. What are you asking me for? The Twin Cities! I don't know! You and your sister are too damn spoiled. You wanna give me some help here?

GENE. What do you want?

NICK. Lay the table. Feed your mother.

GENE. She doesn't want me feeding her!

NICK. You do it too fast. Let her chew, for Christ's sake! You let it all go down her chin, of course she doesn't like it.

GENE. She doesn't like me doing it, she doesn't like me…
[doing it.]

NICK. It's because you don't pay attention.

NICK *is checking his watch with the clock on the wall.
Underscore begins for 'Went To See The Gypsy'.*

GENE. What's up your nose all of a sudden?

NICK. What?

GENE. Why you so on edge?

NICK. I'm not on edge.

GENE. No, huh?

MRS NEILSEN, *a woman in her early forties, comes into
focus. She wears a skirt with pockets in it. When she has her
hands in her pockets she takes on a kind of lounging
adolescent rebelliousness. She sings.*

Went To See The Gypsy

Went to see the gypsy
Stayin' in a big hotel
He smiled when he saw me coming
And he said, 'Well, well, well'
His room was dark and crowded
Lights were low and dim
'How are you?' he said to me
I said it back to him

I went down to the lobby
To make a small call out
A pretty dancing girl was there
And she began to shout
'Go on back to see the gypsy
He can move you from the rear
Drive you from your fear
Bring you through the mirror
He did it in Las Vegas
And he can do it here'

> Outside the lights were shining
> On the river of tears
> I watched them from the distance
> With music in my ears

NICK. Mrs Neilsen.

MRS NEILSEN. Mr Laine. How are you all this evening?

NICK. All fine, thank you.

MRS NEILSEN. Gene.

GENE. Mrs Neilsen.

NICK. We have chicken stew if you're hungry.

MRS NEILSEN. It smells very good.

GENE *slips away.* NICK *tries to feed a reluctant* ELIZABETH.

NICK. I fixed that window was banging in your room.

MRS NEILSEN. I saw that, thank you. Wind's picking up.

NICK. There's a storm due.

MRS NEILSEN. It's making it rattle a little.

NICK. Oh?

MRS NEILSEN *watches* NICK *tidy up a little.*

MRS NEILSEN. You want to come and fix it tonight?

NICK. I don't know. I'm…

MRS NEILSEN. Fix my window.

MRS NEILSEN *tries to touch him playfully.*

NICK (*whispers*). Not in front of Elizabeth, alright?

MRS NEILSEN. She's not watching.

NICK (*doubtfully*). Yeah…

MRS NEILSEN *puts her newspaper where he can see it.*

MRS NEILSEN. You see this one?

NICK *glances at it. Looks at her.*

NICK. You could afford that?

MRS NEILSEN. Depends, I guess. But look at it. It's got a real restaurant. Twenty-two rooms. We could whip it into shape.

NICK. Twenty-two rooms, huh?

MRS NEILSEN. We could handle it. With your experience and my charisma.

NICK. Yeah. Up in Bismark…

MRS NEILSEN. You don't like Bismark?

NICK. Guy I knew from Bismark always cheated at cards.

MRS NEILSEN (*whipping newspaper away*). Oh right, what was I thinking?

NICK. Don't get sore! It's a great idea. I just wish I could think straight.

MRS NEILSEN. What's to think about? You got some other plan?

NICK. Your money comes through, I'll be full a plans.

MRS NEILSEN. It'll come through. Don't be so pessimistic.

NICK. Yeah, I know. Just… Bismark…

She sees him checking his watch.

MRS NEILSEN. What are you up to?

NICK. I'm not up to nothing.

MRS NEILSEN. Why do you keep looking at your watch?

NICK. Do I? Just wondering. Where Marianne is.

MRS NEILSEN. She's a grown woman.

NICK. She has a baby inside her! Can't be traipsing up and down the streets! In the cold. (*Pause.*) Mr Perry's calling by, and…

MRS NEILSEN. The shoe mender?

NICK. Mm hm.

MRS NEILSEN. For what?

NICK. He's a good man.

MRS NEILSEN. So?

NICK (*as though* MRS NEILSEN *is missing something very obvious*). So…

MRS NEILSEN. He must be seventy if he's a day!

NICK. He's not seventy!

MRS NEILSEN. So what is he? Sixty-nine and a half? The girl is nineteen!

NICK (*shrugs*). She needs a husband.

MRS NEILSEN. What for?

NICK. Take care of her. The father's jumped on a damn lake boat – probably down in Toledo by now.

MRS NEILSEN. Maybe she doesn't need a husband.

NICK. Oh yeah? Well where's she gonna go?

MRS NEILSEN. Why does she have to go anywhere?

NICK. Because… it's… (*Suddenly changes tack, picking on* MRS NEILSEN *irritably.*) What do you care? When your probate comes through, you know what you'll do? You'll just get back on the train and go back to Minneapolis – and why shouldn't you?

MRS NEILSEN (*rising to his irritable tone*). Well I can't live in a boarding house forever, can I? (*Indicates* ELIZABETH.) With your wife!

Now they are arguing.

NICK. With my what? She was finished with me anyway!

MRS NEILSEN. So *you* say.

NICK. Before she got sick! She told me straight out.

MRS NEILSEN. Yeah…

NICK. And now she's just forgotten! When someone turns round just says, 'I don't love you any more', you know what the shock is? There ain't nothing you can do! That's it! You

can't make 'em love ya. People love dirtbags all over the
world – even name the damn children after 'em! Doesn't
mean anyone's gotta love you.

MRS NEILSEN. Well maybe someone does, Nick – you ever
thought a that?

She turns away and sits at the table to eat.

Segue back to 'Went To See The Gypsy'.

Went To See The Gypsy

I went back to see the gypsy
It was nearly early dawn
The gypsy's door was open wide
But the gypsy was gone
And that pretty dancing girl
She could not be found
So I watched that sun come rising
From that little Minnesota town

Outside, a man in his sixties, MR PERRY, *carries a bunch of
flowers up to the porch.*

He rings the bell.

MRS NEILSEN. You're not finished with her, Nick.

NICK (*unconvinced*). Yeah?

MRS NEILSEN. You don't know it?

NICK. I don't know nothing no more.

GENE *brings in* PERRY. NICK *and* MRS NEILSEN *spring
apart. But surely* GENE *has seen them.*

Mr Perry.

PERRY. Mr Laine.

NICK. Come in, come in.

PERRY. Why, thank you.

NICK. You know Mrs Neilsen.

PERRY. I've seen you.

MRS NEILSEN. Yes, we've… (*Indicates 'seen each other'*.)

NICK. Mrs Neilsen is a guest here. She… has business here… When her business is done she'll be…

PERRY. Well I hope you find Duluth to be as hospitable as we suppose it to be?

MRS NEILSEN. It's a fine, beautiful city.

PERRY. Yes, well we like to think so.

NICK. Gene of course, you know.

PERRY *smiles at* GENE.

And Elizabeth.

PERRY. Of course. How are you this evening, Mrs Laine?

ELIZABETH *smiles knowingly at him*.

NICK (*perturbed by* ELIZABETH's *expression*). And I… Gene, where's Marianne?

GENE. I don't know.

NICK. Will you see if maybe she came in please? Will you look in her room?

GENE *goes*.

Well… There's a stormy night!

PERRY. Yes. (*Pause*.) I swore I'd make it up that hill.

They laugh as if this is a good joke, to hide their discomfort.

NICK. It's a-blowin'!

Strained smiles from PERRY *and* MRS NEILSEN.

You take a drink? A glass of beer?

PERRY. A glass of milk would be…

NICK. Right!

NICK *starts to go but* MRS NEILSEN *heads him off. Anything to get out of the room.*

MRS NEILSEN. I'll get it.

She goes to the kitchen.

NICK. How's the… How's the shoe-mending business? If that's not a personal question.

PERRY. Not at all. My store is full of shoes. I'm occupied from daybreak till dark. Thank the Lord.

NICK. You're occupied.

PERRY. Yes, sir.

NICK. How long has it been since your wife passed?

PERRY. Twelve years.

NICK. Twelve years, huh?

PERRY. That's right.

NICK. That's uh…

PERRY. Yeah, it's a long time I guess.

NICK. Twelve years is a long time. It's a chunk of change.

PERRY. Well.

MRS NEILSEN *comes back with a glass of milk.*

Oh, thank you.

ELIZABETH. You're welcome.

NICK. You know how Marianne came to be our daughter, right?

PERRY. I heard something…

NICK. Someone checked out – left a bag on the bed and you know what was in it?

ELIZABETH. Marianne!

NICK. Marianne! She was only a baby. I mean we tried to find the parents. Seemed the best thing was to let her stay here. Elizabeth took care of her. No one ever came back.

PERRY. You're good people.

NICK. I don't know. I guess. Elizabeth always wanted a daughter.

ELIZABETH. We lost a baby girl.

PERRY *smiles at* ELIZABETH *who looks at* PERRY *inscrutably.*

NICK (*desperate for something to say*). Mrs Neilsen is a widow.

MRS NEILSEN *winces at this label, but smiles through it.*

PERRY. Oh, I am sorry.

MRS NEILSEN. Thank you.

NICK. She was up in St Paul.

PERRY. I see.

NICK. Husband died three years ago, she's still waiting on his will to be cleared!

PERRY. Oh.

NICK. Charles St Clair, here in Duluth…

PERRY. Mm-hm.

NICK. He's doing the paperwork. It'll get cleared out. She's got a favorable rate here and it'll all…

Behind PERRY*'s back*, MRS NEILSEN *kicks* NICK.

PERRY. Oh I'm sure.

MRS NEILSEN. Yes.

MRS NEILSEN *smiles through gritted teeth.*

PERRY. Your husband have ties here?

MRS NEILSEN. He was in the railroad business. He had shares in the line.

PERRY (*impressed*). Right…

MRS NEILSEN. They have all the right paperwork now. It won't take long. And then I'll…

PERRY. You'll buy a house here in Duluth.

MRS NEILSEN (*a little too quickly*). No. I'll…

NICK. She'll spread her wings.

ELIZABETH. Are those flowers for me?

PERRY looks at the flowers. NICK looks, aghast, at
ELIZABETH.

NICK. Now, Elizabeth…

ELIZABETH. They're pretty.

PERRY. Well, they're for eh… why, well, yes, they're…
They're for you.

She doesn't take them.

ELIZABETH. Can you remember? When you asked me and
asked me and asked me to come with you to the Cook
County fair?

PERRY smiles, unsure what to say.

NICK. Well now, Elizabeth, I'm sure that wasn't Mr Perry…

ELIZABETH. Can you remember? The lights? And how dark it
was afterwards walking home together and what you said to
me? Begging me to touch it?

NICK. Elizabeth, now, please!

ELIZABETH. 'For the love of mercy, please just hold it,
Elizabeth,' you said.

PERRY. Well now I…

ELIZABETH. 'Just hold it. Just touch it. I'm begging you.' Do
you remember?

NICK. For Christ's sake, Elizabeth… I'm sorry, Mr Perry.

ELIZABETH. And I said, 'Why, it's just like a tiny Vienna
sausage!'

NICK. I'm so sorry.

ELIZABETH. How I cried afterwards – I was only a girl.

NICK grabs her roughly.

NICK. Elizabeth!

ELIZABETH *hits back at him just as* MARIANNE *comes through the door.* PERRY *stands there awkwardly with his flowers.*

NICK. Marianne! You're… Look who's here.

PERRY. Good evening, Marianne.

MARIANNE. Mr Perry.

NICK. Well I'm… (*Stretches, yawns.*) We should really start getting Elizabeth to bed. Mrs Neilsen, would you mind? I hate to impinge…

MRS NEILSEN (*pointedly to* NICK). Not at all. Come on, Elizabeth, I'll brush your teeth.

ELIZABETH. And sing?

MRS NEILSEN. Sure.

NICK. Marianne, you'll… (*Nods repeatedly at* MARIANNE *to make her stay.*) I'll just…

NICK *follows* ELIZABETH *and* MRS NEILSEN *out, leaving* MARIANNE *and* PERRY *alone.* PERRY *still holds his flowers and his milk.*

PERRY. Well, this is nice. (*Pause.*) You are finished your schooling now I believe.

MARIANNE. Yes, sir.

PERRY. Now, Marianne. I'm going to be frank with you. Your father has spoken with me and I am aware of your… I am aware of your condition. My house is warm, it's centrally located. My habits are regular. I will wed you, Marianne, and parent the child.

MARIANNE. Mr Perry, your offer is very kind but…

PERRY (*talks over her*). I'm a deal older than you. I may not look it, but it's true. I won't be round for ever. Time comes, you'll have the whole place. Child'll be reared, and you'll be free – and still a relatively young woman. Now there's a deal and if I ever heard better it's gone from my mind.

MARIANNE. Mr Perry, I can't.

PERRY. It's a lot to take in. I get it. I really do. But you sleep on it.

MARIANNE. Mr Perry, I...

She goes to speak again but he silences her.

PERRY. You sleep on it! Inspiration comes in dreams!

He leaves.

MARIANNE *sings.*

Tight Connection To My Heart (Has Anyone Seen My Love)

Well, I had to move fast
And I couldn't with you around my neck
I said I'd send for you and I did
What did you expect?
My hands are sweating
And we haven't even started yet
I'll go along with the charade
Until I can think my way out
I know it was all a big joke
Whatever it was about
Someday maybe
I'll remember to forget

I'm gonna get my coat
I feel the breath of a storm
There's something I've got to do tonight
You go inside and stay warm

Has anybody seen my love
Has anybody seen my love
Has anybody seen my love
I don't know
Has anybody seen my love?

You want to talk to me
Go ahead and talk
Whatever you got to say to me
Won't come as any shock
I must be guilty of something

You just whisper it into my ear
Madame Butterfly
She lulled me to sleep
In a town without pity
Where the water runs deep
She said, 'Be easy, baby
There ain't nothin' worth stealin' in here'

You're the one I've been looking for
You're the one that's got the key
But I can't figure out whether I'm too good for you
Or you're too good for me

Has anybody seen my love
Has anybody seen my love
Has anybody seen my love
I don't know
Has anybody seen my love?

As the music ends, some hours have passed. It's the middle of the night. Rain pours down outside and wind blows. There is a loud thumping at the front door. NICK *comes down through the house.*

NICK. Alright! Alright!

He opens the door to two men. A middle-aged white man, REVEREND MARLOWE, *and a young athletic-looking black man,* JOE SCOTT.

MARLOWE. Sir, I am the Reverend James Marlowe, this young man is Joseph Scott Esquire. The Spalding has no vacancies. They recommended your fine house.

NICK. Well come in out of the rain and let's see what we can do. Come on. Through this way.

MARLOWE. Thank you.

SCOTT. Thank you, sir.

NICK *brings the gentlemen in to the dining room.*

NICK. I have a small room in the back, it'll do one of you. Someone can bunk on that settle in here, it makes a decent cot, if you don't mind.

SCOTT. I'll sleep anywhere. A chair is fine for me, sir.

NICK. No, you can stretch on out there. I'll charge you a half-dollar. And let's say a dollar fifty for the room in back for yourself.

MARLOWE. A dollar fifty?

NICK. That's right. It's normally two dollars. But considering it's three thirty in the morning I'll give you a discount. And a half a dollar for the settle here.

NICK stands in front of SCOTT waiting to be paid. SCOTT reaches into his pockets, he counts coins, small pieces of change, into NICK's hand. NICK stands there mercilessly waiting for every penny. He counts it. Satisfied, he turns to MARLOWE who hands him two dollars. NICK instantly sticks MARLOWE with all of SCOTT's change.

And there's your change. Now what do you say you gents have a glass of whiskey?

MARLOWE. Well that would be a godsend.

SCOTT. Thank you, sir.

NICK goes to pour them a drink.

NICK. You can hang those wet coats up yonder.

SCOTT. Yes, sir.

NICK. So, no room at the inn over at The Spalding, huh?

MARLOWE. That's correct.

NICK (*dubious*). Mmm.

MARLOWE. The eleven o'clock from St Paul was delayed.

NICK. You boys travelling together?

MARLOWE. No, sir. We are thrown together by circumstance. Decided to walk on up here together.

NICK. You say you're a reverend?

MARLOWE. That is correct, sir.

NICK. You planning to preach the word?

MARLOWE. I don't preach the word, sir. I sell it. A devil pursues me and his name is commerce.

NICK. You're a Bible salesman?

MARLOWE. In its most basic terms, yes.

NICK. You selling much?

MARLOWE. If I sell two Bibles a day, three, I can live.

NICK. Mind if you don't go selling 'em in here?

MARLOWE. Beneath your roof the word is free.

NICK. That's two bits for the whiskey. You'll find it's the highest quality.

MARLOWE. As the price suggests.

NICK. What's the most you ever owed anybody?

MARLOWE. Excuse me?

NICK *pours himself a big slug of whiskey.*

NICK. What's the most money you ever had to pay back to someone? Twenty thousand dollars?

MARLOWE. Well no, not *that* kind of…

NICK. You try walking round with that kind of money hanging over you, my friend. You try it for a day. See what it's like. You try it for a lifetime. Never ever invest in the fairground business. Those people are… (*Stops himself. To* SCOTT.) How about you?

SCOTT. Sir?

NICK. What's your business?

SCOTT. I have an appointment here.

NICK, *realising that's as much as he'll get, desists.*

NICK. Well alright, there's blankets in there.

NICK *opens a door in the dresser to show* SCOTT *the blankets.*

Come on, Reverend, I'll show you. Goodnight.

SCOTT. Goodnight, sir.

MARLOWE. Goodnight, Mr Scott.

SCOTT. Goodnight, Reverend.

> NICK *takes* MARLOWE *out the back. Alone in the room,*
> SCOTT *takes a blanket and throws it on the settle. He takes*
> *off his outer garments.*
>
> *We see* NICK *going off up to bed.* SCOTT *settles himself,*
> *putting his things away in his bag, etc. The room is dark,*
> *only a little light on somewhere. All is quiet.*
>
> *Suddenly there's a crash out in the kitchen.* SCOTT *turns*
> *round, startled.*

GENE (*from the kitchen, in pain*). Mother-*fucker*!

SCOTT. Who's there?

GENE (*coming through to the dining room*). What?

SCOTT. Who's there?

GENE (*drunkenly*). Who am *I*?

SCOTT. Are you alright?

GENE. Who is that?

SCOTT. Joseph P. Scott, sir.

GENE. You asking me who *I* am? Who are you, boy?

SCOTT. Joseph Scott, sir.

GENE. Uh-huh.

SCOTT. Easy, my man.

GENE. What are you doing in here, boy?

SCOTT. Just stayin' the night. The boss man admitted me
    himself.

GENE. Oh did he, did he, did he? You tryna start something?

SCOTT. No, sir, I just want a night's sleep. I paid for it.

GENE. You think something is funny?

SCOTT. No, sir.

GENE. You had some schooling?

SCOTT. Yes, sir.

GENE. Where? Harvard?

SCOTT. No, sir, Miss Hemming's schoolhouse, sir. 219 Washington St in Brainerd.

GENE. You taking a run at me, boy?

SCOTT. No, sir.

GENE. You come on and hit me now.

SCOTT. Sir?

GENE. Hit me. I said hit me.

SCOTT. No, sir.

GENE. You get your black ass up outta that bed and you stand up and you hit me now. You get up and you hit me.

GENE *pulls at* SCOTT. SCOTT *stands up wearily.*

Come on.

SCOTT. I ain't gonna hit you.

GENE. It's alright. You can do it.

SCOTT. I ain't gonna do it.

GENE. Now I said you come and you hit me now or I'm gonna take this poker and I'm gonna stick it through your goddamn eye.

SCOTT. And I said I ain't gonna hit you.

GENE. I say you do as you are told, boy, or you give me one good reason why I don't make you do it.

SCOTT. 'Cause if I hit you, I'll likely kill you.

Pause.

GENE. What you say?

SCOTT. You heard me.

GENE. Well you done it now.

> GENE *goes to* SCOTT. SCOTT *easily knocks* GENE *down with a blow, sending him reeling back across the room.* GENE *is dazed for a moment, but then sees red, rallies, and charges at* SCOTT. SCOTT *boxes* GENE *into a corner,* GENE *collapses, crumpled to the floor.*

> Alright! Alright! Okay! Okay...

SCOTT. You want me to hit you?

GENE. No.

SCOTT. You want me to hit you some more, boy?

GENE. No.

SCOTT. Huh?

GENE. No.

SCOTT. No what?

GENE. No, sir.

SCOTT. No what?

GENE. No I don't want you to hit me any more.

> MARLOWE *comes in wearing his waistcoat and shirt.*

MARLOWE. Now there's a man looks like he could use a Bible.

> SCOTT *moves away from* GENE. MARLOWE *goes and gets himself a drink from* NICK*'s whiskey bottle.* GENE *picks himself up.*

> James Marlowe. Reverend Jim they call me.

GENE. Right.

MARLOWE. You live here?

> GENE *barely responds. His nose is bleeding. He rubs at it, seeing blood on his hand.*

SCOTT. Where's the convenience?

GENE *indicates where the bathroom is*, SCOTT *goes out, stopping at* GENE *on the way.*

Goddamn, man, what the hell?

GENE *just looks away as* SCOTT *goes.*

MARLOWE. I just saw you stroke a cat out there on your way in through the backyard. Cat rubbed its fur round your legs like he's the only friend you got in the world. And you know what I thought to myself? What are you gonna do when that cat dies? Have you thought about it? Have you considered death?

GENE *gets himself a drink. Percussive rhythm begins for 'Slow Train'.*

GENE. What you say? You're a reverend, huh?

GENE *is not interested. He gets himself another drink.*

MARLOWE. Yes, sir. The word of God, sir, cloth-bound, gold-embossed, extra-fine print for a mere two dollars. Jesus makes his lifetime of light eminently affordable. Big storm's coming, my boy. Here. Europe. Everywhere. You ever wonder what woulda happened if the Jews met the Vikings? Huh? The Vikings! You know what they woulda done to the Jews?

GENE. I ain't got two dollars.

SCOTT *comes back. He gives* GENE *a handkerchief to clean himself up.* GENE *dabs at the blood on his face.*

MARLOWE. A fine young man like you? Something's wrong somewhere when a fine man like you ain't got two damn dollars – dontcha feel it? Keep it.

MARLOWE *pours some whiskey in* GENE's *glass as music starts.* MARLOWE *and* SCOTT *sing.*

Slow Train

Sometimes I feel so low-down and disgusted
Can't help but wonder what's happenin' to my companions
Are they lost or are they found
Have they counted the cost it'll take to bring down
All their earthly principles they're gonna have to abandon?
There's a slow, slow train comin' up around the bend

I had a woman down in Alabama
She was a backwoods girl, but she sure was realistic
She said, 'Boy, without a doubt
Have to quit your mess and straighten out
You could die down here, be just another accident statistic'
There's a slow, slow train comin' up around the bend

...

Man's ego is inflated, his laws are outdated, they don't
      apply no more
You can't rely no more to be standin' around waitin'
In the home of the brave
Jefferson turnin' over in his grave
Fools glorifying themselves, trying to manipulate Satan
And there's a slow, slow train comin' up around the bend

...

Well, my baby went to Illinois with some bad-talkin' boy
      she could destroy
A real suicide case, but there was nothin' I could do to
      stop it
I don't care about economy
I don't care about astronomy
But it sure do bother me to see my loved ones turning into
      puppets
There's a slow, slow train comin' up around the bend

Segue to 'License To Kill'. MRS NEILSEN, MARIANNE,
KATE *and company sing*.

License To Kill

> …
>
> Now, there's a woman on my block
> She just sit there as the night grows still
> She say who gonna take away his license to kill?
>
> Now, they take him and they teach him and they groom
>   him for life
> And they set him on a path where he's bound to get ill
> Then they bury him with stars
> Sell his body like they do used cars
>
> Now, there's a woman on my block
> She just sit there facin' the hill
> She say who gonna take away his license to kill?

They segue back to 'Slow Train'.

During the last verse, GENE *and* MARLOWE *have retired to their rooms,* SCOTT *has lain on the settle. The light changes, bringing us to morning.* MARIANNE *comes through the kitchen, carrying breakfast things to the table.* ELIZABETH *comes in with her.* SCOTT *turns over.* MARIANNE *halts.*

ELIZABETH. Hey!

MARIANNE. Oh I'm sorry.

SCOTT. No, ma'am.

MARIANNE. I'll let you get up.

SCOTT. That's alright. I'm dressed.

> SCOTT *gets up, still wearing his clothes.*

MARIANNE. Would you like some breakfast?

SCOTT. Yes thank you.

MARIANNE. The guests like oatmeal. You like it?

SCOTT. Yes, ma'am.

MARIANNE. Coffee is on the way.

SCOTT. What's your name?

MARIANNE. Marianne Laine.

SCOTT. Joseph Scott.

She comes and shakes his hand. He goes to ELIZABETH.

Joseph Scott, ma'am.

ELIZABETH *just gives him a vague smile.*

MARIANNE. This is my mama. She might say something. She mightn't. She's... [not herself.]

SCOTT. Pleased to meet you, ma'am.

MARIANNE. You in Duluth for long?

SCOTT. No. Couple days, then I head down to Chicago.

MARIANNE. Chicago huh?

SCOTT. You been there?

MARIANNE. No.

SCOTT. Well you should go some day. It's worth seeing.

MARIANNE. I will.

Down the hall, NICK *admits* DR WALKER *to the house.*

DR WALKER. Morning, Nick, How are you?

NICK (*holds out his arms*). You tell me, right?

DR WALKER. You're okay.

NICK. Look who it is, Elizabeth. Doc coming by to see you.

ELIZABETH *embraces* DR WALKER.

DR WALKER. Well there's a welcome you don't get every day.

NICK. She can still spot a good 'un. Breakfast?

DR WALKER. No thank you.

NICK. Come on down for coffee.

DR WALKER. No – just wanted to drop in Elizabeth's prescription.

NICK. I'd a come by to get it, you didn't need to do that. Come in, have a coffee.

DR WALKER. Well alright.

They meet MR *and* MRS BURKE *arriving down for breakfast with their son,* ELIAS.

ELIAS *is in his thirties but has the mental age of a four-year-old child.* MRS BURKE *is a wiry strong woman and her husband is a balding rotund man. She carries an air of determination. He carries one of defeat, but he doesn't know that.*

MR BURKE. Morning, Doc.

DR WALKER. Folks.

MARIANNE *turns on the wireless. A 1930s style arrangement of 'Tonight I'll Be Staying Here With You' is playing.*

MR BURKE. Good morning.

SCOTT. Good morning, sir.

MR BURKE. Frank Burke, this is my wife Laura, my son, Elias.

SCOTT. Joe Scott. Pleased to meet you.

MR BURKE. Dr Walker.

SCOTT. Sir.

MR BURKE. Mrs Neilsen.

SCOTT. Ma'am.

ELIAS. Mommy, my scarecrow – (*Searching for a word.*) ah, ah, ah, ah… My scarecrow, ah, ah, ah, my scarecrow wears a hat.

ELIZABETH. What the fuck is wrong with you?

MRS BURKE. Mrs Neilsen.

NICK *passes through, carrying tools, doing some maintenance work.*

NICK. Marianne, get some coffee for Dr Walker.

MRS NEILSEN. Now, Mr Laine. Did you hear that? Elias's scarecrow wears a hat, no less.

NICK. I did hear that. Yes, and I saw your scarecrow this morning, Elias. He's looking fine and hardy. Those are some nice twigs you stuck in his… in his head.

MRS BURKE *brings* ELIAS *to the table. Breakfast is underway, with* MARIANNE *bringing things in and out and everyone helping themselves. During the following,* NICK *is hammering nails in a shutter somewhere. Sometimes people have to shout over the din.*

MARIANNE *brings* DR WALKER *some coffee. But she doesn't make eye contact with him.*

MR BURKE. Please correct me if I'm wrong. Haven't I seen you fight, sir?

SCOTT. Oh?

MR BURKE. Saw you knock out Frazier Fitch in Hubertsville May 1928, am I right?

SCOTT. That's right, sir.

MR BURKE. You're quite a talent. I lost a lot of money that night.

MRS BURKE. Now, Francis, that's your own fault.

MR BURKE. I'm paying him a compliment, my dear.

SCOTT. Thank you, sir.

MR BURKE. You been fighting much?

SCOTT. Well not so much.

MARLOWE *comes in, dressed.*

MARLOWE. Good morning, all. Good morning. James Marlowe.

MR BURKE. Frank Burke. My wife, Laura, Elias. Mrs Laine over there, Mrs Neilsen.

MARLOWE. Pleased to meet you.

MR BURKE. This young man is Jungle Joe Scott. You know who he is?

MARLOWE. Why yes! We've been acquainted since last night.

MR BURKE. So you know – very talented young man.

MARLOWE. Oh? Not that I'm surprised.

MR BURKE. A rising young man of the pugilistic arts. You been fighting much?

MARLOWE *watches as* ELIZABETH *finds a coin on the floor and puts it in her little box under her chair.*

SCOTT. Oh not so much.

MR BURKE. Well that's a pity. You should.

SCOTT. Well, I wasn't really able to.

MR BURKE. You injured?

SCOTT. No, I…

MR BURKE. 'Cause a talent like that shouldn't go to waste. No talent should.

MARLOWE (*helping himself to coffee*). Well you know, a man can lose his nerve.

MR BURKE. That can happen, too. You travel round so much, you lose your bearings, you lose the hunger.

MARLOWE. You lose the hunger, Mr Scott?

SCOTT. No I…

MARLOWE. You get hurt?

SCOTT. No.

MARLOWE. It's alright to run away.

MR BURKE. Well I don't mean to pry. I admire you, sir.

SCOTT. No it's alright, I can tell you. I was incarcerated up in the Stillwater penitentiary for three years.

MR BURKE. Oh, well that's…

SCOTT. A felon, name of Crawford, claimed he saw me running from a robbery there April 15th 1929, however his testimony was withdrawn in January this year before a court who declared my conviction to be unsound.

MR BURKE. Well congratulations.

SCOTT. Thank you.

MARLOWE. Well Halleluiah.

ELIZABETH. Well, Halleluiah.

MRS BURKE. What an ordeal.

*The music on the wireless segues into a 1930s arrangement
of 'Dear Landlord'.*

SCOTT. Yes, ma'am. For a man who never smoked, to be stuck
inside with men who just burned cigarettes all night. That
was maybe the worst part somehow. And the shame of
course. For my family.

MRS BURKE. It's terrible.

MR BURKE. You must be itching to get back in the game. You
get compensation?

SCOTT. No, sir. I been living under a bridge up in St Paul.
A newspaper gentleman named Mose McCabe forwarded me
a little money, recommended I talk to a man down here
named Mr Murphy might invest in a comeback. But now
I hear he's down in Chicago so I'll make my way down there.

MR BURKE. Sir, I admire your initiative and your tenacity and
goddamn if there isn't a tear in my eye. And I don't know who
this Mr Murphy is but I would like to offer you, right here and
right now, my services as a manager – or a partner or…

MRS BURKE. Francis…

MR BURKE. Well why not? It's a business. And if there's one
thing I know – it's business.

ELIAS *emits a long, high-pitched sigh.*

MRS BURKE. Yes, you know it too well.

*She means this as a sort of joke, but he takes it hard,
humiliated before the company.*

MR BURKE. What's that supposed to mean?

MRS BURKE. Well let's just say it's an acquaintanceship that
has not treated you and business equally.

MR BURKE (*laughing but really appealing for reason*).
Woman, a man walks in here and I decide to discuss an
opportunity – you cannot wait two moments before you
deride me!

MRS BURKE. You can't manage your own son or provide for
your wife and you want tell a stranger you'll manage his
affairs – with what? From where? Working out of a closet in
a two-bit flophouse?!

ELIAS *starts blowing on a harmonica. His parents shout
over the din.*

MR BURKE. An operation like this? That's the beauty of it!

MRS BURKE. Beauty's in the eye of the beholder.

MR BURKE. It *is* beautiful! It *is* beautiful! Jesus Christ! Elias!
Not at table!

MR BURKE *grabs the harmonica roughly.*

*The band take over from the wireless. Their underscore
echoes 'Ballad Of A Thin Man', 'Dear Landlord', snatches
of 'I Want You'...*

DR WALKER *addresses us.*

DR WALKER. Marianne had a lonely upbringing.

To say it wasn't fashionable in Minnesota to bring up a black
child in a white family in those days would be an
understatement. In 1920, when Marianne was just five years
old, three black men named Isaac McGhie, Elmer Jackson,
and Elias Clayton were lynched by a mob who broke into the
jail, right here in Duluth. Hanged 'em down on the corner of
1st Street for a crime they hadn't committed. No one was
ever even prosecuted for it.

Nick didn't want to be seen holding a little black girl's hand
going down to school, so Elizabeth taught her everything she
knew right here in the house.

Nick didn't like it one bit when Marianne started going
around other parts of the town. Looking for music, for life.
But what could he do?

When Nick was ten years old he was asked to mind his little sister for the day. She was six. Her name was Leonora. This was up in Rocheleau – lotta mining up there. Nick had arranged with his friends to fight another gang of boys up in the woods. He took Leonora with him – she fell down a taconite hole. Fell forty feet. The boys could hear her down there – calling out for Nick. But by the time help came… (*Opens his hands.*) Nick was sent down here to live with his granddaddy. It was one of those stories you hear about people, you think about it every time you look in their face.

It's pouring rain. MARIANNE *is on the front porch smoking.* GENE *comes out to her.*

GENE. Hey.

MARIANNE. Hey.

GENE. Whatcha doin?

MARIANNE. Watchin' the birds.

GENE. What birds?

MARIANNE. The mama and the baby.

GENE. There ain't no babies in November.

MARIANNE. She's got one.

GENE. Maybe it never grew.

MARIANNE. Maybe. You wanna see a movie?

GENE. What's on?

MARIANNE. You see *It Happened One Night*?

GENE. Who's in it?

MARIANNE. Clark Gable. It's goofy. This guy is helping this girl run away from getting married.

He smiles mischievously at her.

GENE. You'd go and see it again?

MARIANNE. Sure if you wanna… I got nothin' to wear.

GENE. You can wear my sweater.

MARIANNE (*unimpressed*). Right…

GENE. Who's lookin' at you?

MARIANNE *looks at him*.

You ever gonna tell me?

MARIANNE. What.

He looks at her belly.

Don't ask me, Gene, alright?

They go quiet as NICK *approaches*.

NICK. Hey! Gene! The hell happened to your face?

GENE. Someone thought I had their lottery ticket.

NICK. Did ya?

GENE. I wish!

NICK *gives* GENE *a letter*.

What's this?

NICK. Read it.

GENE. What is it?

NICK. Appointment for an interview.

GENE. Interview for what?

NICK. Lake Superior and Mississippi Railroad. Right here.

GENE. Yeah, what is it? Punching tickets?

NICK. What do you care? You know what other guys'd do just to get in the door? Just to sweep the damn platform? I ain't gonna tell you the favors I had to pull. Had to sweet-talk an old girlfriend.

GENE. I don't wanna hear that!

NICK. You kids don't think I was young once? You think I was born like this? Like an old man! You have no idea, my friend.

GENE. Yeah, well that's got nothin' to do with me.

NICK. No, huh? And I got nothin' to do with you?

GENE. Mostly you don't.

NICK (*offended*). I don't have nothing to do with you?

GENE. Why the sudden interest?

NICK. I can't take an interest in you?

GENE. Sure, I guess.

NICK. Well there you go.

GENE. What you up to?

NICK. I'm not up to anything.

GENE. I don't get it.

NICK. I want for you to make money.

GENE. Alright.

NICK. You get it?

GENE. Kinda.

NICK. You do this for me, okay? You do it for me, you do it for
    your mother, you do your best. (*Pause.*) What?

GENE. Nothing.

NICK. Hm?

GENE. Nothing.

NICK. You go to that interview.

> *A girl in her twenties,* KATE, *approaches the porch, she
> holds an umbrella against the teeming rain.* GENE *is lost for
> words for a moment.*

KATE. Morning, Mr Laine.

NICK. Morning, Kate. How's your mother?

KATE. Well, thank you.

NICK. And your father?

KATE. He's well too.

NICK. Well that's…

NICK *and* MARIANNE *go*.

GENE. Kate…

KATE. I hope it's alright – calling by like this.

GENE. No! Hey… Come in.

KATE. I can't stay.

GENE. Hey, that's alright. You want some breakfast?

KATE. No, thank you, I'm fine.

GENE. Cup of coffee?

KATE. I can't. I have a ticket for the nine o'clock Greyhound – to Boston.

GENE (*steps into the rain, holding a newspaper over his head*). You going to Boston?

KATE. I got a job. Teaching. For a family. It's kind of a governess.

GENE. Great.

KATE. Three girls.

GENE. Wow. That's terrif…

KATE. Jed Simons has asked me to marry him, Gene. I've said yes.

Short pause.

GENE. Wo… Wow that's… That's great.

KATE. I wanted to tell you myself. You know how these things…

GENE. I know. That's… That can be really… thank you.

KATE. Are you okay?

GENE. I'm great. I'm… why wouldn't I…?

KATE. What happened to your face?

GENE. Oh this! No, I… damn branch on that sycamore tree sprung back and hit me while was, tryna… chop it down.

KATE (*looking at his face, concerned*). Did you clean it?

GENE. I gotta clean it. I'll do it.

KATE. If I had time I'd…

GENE. No, no, I know, I'll do it. I know. So, Boston!

KATE. Yeah.

GENE. That's great.

KATE. Yeah it's… You know Jed is gonna be working out there.

GENE. Yeah, I heard something… That's…

KATE. Gene, I'm sorry about what I said to you…

GENE. When?

KATE. You know…

GENE. Oh, hey, no. Don't. I deserved it.

KATE. I do admire you, Gene. I always have. I can feel there's so many great things you could do. I guess I got angry and I…

GENE. Kate, I was drunk. I was drunk and I… You know what? When we're old and we're like fifty years old and we look back at this whole thing, you know what? I bet we're just gonna laugh our damn heads off about the whole thing. I'm even laughing right now. It's funny!

KATE. I better go, Gene.

GENE. You better go, Kate. And you know what?

KATE. Yeah?

Pause.

GENE. Nothin'.

KATE *starts to go, she turns back.*

KATE. I wanted to give you back this, Gene. I nearly forgot. It's your mother's St Christopher medal.

GENE. Keep it!

KATE. No I couldn't.

GENE. Really.

KATE. It's your mother's.

GENE. No keep it. Really. She won't care!

KATE. I couldn't.

GENE (*losing his temper*). I said keep it! I said keep it!

He shoves it roughly in her hand.

I don't want it. You understand me? I don't want it!

KATE, *confused, holds on to it and moves away. Bare chords for 'I Want You' begin under the following.*

(*Regaining composure.*) I'll see you, Kate. You take care.

KATE. Okay.

GENE (*calls to her*). I have an interview.

KATE (*turning*). Oh?

GENE. Yeah, Lake Superior and Mississippi Railroad.

KATE. Oh that's wonderful.

GENE. Yeah. They say I should making three thousand dollars by this time next year.

KATE. Really?

GENE. Sure.

KATE doesn't really believe him, but smiles and starts to go.

You wanna see the letter?

KATE. No that's fine.

GENE. You tell Jed!

KATE. I will.

She turns away. GENE watches her. As music starts and they sing, they could dance and even kiss. We see what their souls are doing despite everything that's just been said. The whole company can sing parts too.

I Want You

The guilty undertaker sighs
The lonesome organ grinder cries
The silver saxophones say I should refuse you
The cracked bells and washed-out horns
Blow into my face with scorn
But it's not that way
I wasn't born to lose you

I want you, I want you
I want you so bad
Honey, I want you

The drunken politician leaps
Upon the street where mothers weep
And the saviors who are fast asleep, they wait for you
And I wait for them to interrupt
Me drinkin' from my broken cup
And ask me to
Open up the gate for you

I want you, I want you
I want you so bad
Honey, I want you

How all my fathers, they've gone down
True love they've been without it
But all their daughters put me down
'Cause I don't think about it

Well, I return to the Queen of Spades
And talk with my chambermaid
She knows that I'm not afraid to look at her
She is good to me
And there's nothing she doesn't see
She knows where I'd like to be
But it doesn't matter

I want you, I want you
I want you so bad
Honey, I want you

MARLOWE *comes into the dining room looking for something to write with.* ELIZABETH *is there wearing sunglasses.*

ELIZABETH. So you're God's representative on Earth, huh?

MARLOWE. Oh no… I'm a mere servant of the servant. Can I serve you?

ELIZABETH. You can't scratch this itch, Padre. I been a long time on the prairie.

MARLOWE. Well you let me know. What you keep all down in here, under your seat there?

ELIZABETH. It's an escape hatch.

MARLOWE. I see.

ELIZABETH. Day's gonna come we all gotta blow.

MARLOWE. Well maybe you'll show me the way out.

ELIZABETH. Everybody gotta go a different door, Monsignor.

MARLOWE. Well maybe that's so.

ELIZABETH. You get a wash this morning?

MARLOWE. Well of course.

ELIZABETH. You might need to go another rinse. It don't smell so sweet down here in the downwind.

MARLOWE. Well perhaps I need to find a laundry.

ELIZABETH. Yeah, well you find a good one. I don't need no louses. I seen one walking down the parting in my hair when I was fixing myself one day. There he was just strolling along the white-line parting like it was a nice country lane, as peaceful and serene… I knew it then, Lord Jesus, I knew it then. I wasn't coming back. (*Beat.*) I can see a louse. I can see 'em.

She is looking pointedly at MARLOWE. MR BURKE *comes in with* ELIAS. *They have a fishing rod.*

MARLOWE. You going fishing? Looks cold out there!

MR BURKE. Elias likes to try. We hardly ever catch anything. Once or twice we had some supper out of it.

One of the guides on the rod is missing. MR BURKE *finds a little wire in a bowl to fix it.*

MARLOWE. That's a fine boy you got there, Mr Burke.

MR BURKE. Thank you. He's a handful. Aren't you?

ELIAS. You gotta ah, ah, ah, put seaweed in the jar so the fish can breathe.

MR BURKE. That's right. It's what we do anyway. Bits of grass, you know.

MARLOWE. Sweet. That's very sweet. You plan on putting some roots down here or you just passing through?

MR BURKE. I guess we'll be moving on. I came down here chasing a debtor gave me the runaround. Everybody chasing everybody else. You know how it is.

MARLOWE. You have creditors on your heels too?

MR BURKE. Everybody got to wait in line, just like everybody else.

MARLOWE. I spent time up in your neck of the woods.

MR BURKE. Uh-huh?

MARLOWE. Wasn't much hunger for the word, but by Christ were they ravenous for something just the same!

MR BURKE. I guess.

Through the following, we hear underscore for 'Blind Willie McTell'.

MARLOWE. Yes it was last spring. I heard a terrible story. About a poor girl's getting attacked up in the woods. Suspicion fell here and there. Some said this, some said that. Someone even said maybe it was a man or child didn't know their own strength. Maybe was a little feeble in his mind. Who can say? You know how it is with rumors. A family by the name of Shepherd. You hear anything about that?

MR BURKE. No, can't say I have.

MARLOWE. These things can happen so easily. I once officiated at a funeral for an infant whose own mother had crushed him to death with an overly fervent embrace. Can you imagine?

MR BURKE. That's terrible.

MARLOWE. Life is terrible.

MR BURKE. It sure can be.

MARLOWE. But you and your wife seem united. And that's the main thing, I guess.

MR BURKE. What you driving at?

MARLOWE. I ain't out to cause trouble. World's already full of trouble. But like they say there's a man going round with his wife and his grown son saying he lost his business. Maybe that's just what he's saying. Maybe he's been moving round 'cause he's got something to hide.

MR BURKE. You're in the wrong garden, preacher.

MARLOWE. Maybe. But I got to be where I am. Just like the next man. Five hundred dollars should do it. Say five o'clock. You meet me here, fine. If not, I'll call by the precinct. Just tell 'em what I know. Look at that! The sun's coming out.

MR BURKE *grabs* MARLOWE.

MR BURKE. Now you listen to me, you son of a bitch. You want to threaten people, you want to get your due, I'll give it to you. You so much as say a goddamn word about me to anyone, I'll cut your fucking throat. You keep your lies to yourself. I don't know a damn thing what you're talking about.

MARLOWE *extricates himself.*

MARLOWE. Then what you getting so riled up about? Huh? If you're unable to hold a decent conversation in a public place maybe you shouldn't have a vulnerable individual in your charge. Maybe you need to think about that till tomorrow. Before you go throwing aspersions around.

Good day. I'm famished. Five o'clock tomorrow. You enjoy your fishing, Elias.

MARLOWE *puts on his hat and leaves.* MR BURKE *angrily takes the fishing rod from* ELIAS.

MR BURKE. What you doing? Gimme that! Look! You took 'em all off! Goddamn...

ELIAS *sits quietly for a moment, then his face contorts and he silently cries.* MR BURKE *sees him.*

Hey, that's alright. Daddy didn't mean to shout. That's alright.

He holds ELIAS. ELIZABETH *just watches, then switches on the wireless. A big band play a version of 'Like A Rolling Stone'.*

I'm sorry. I'm sorry. I love you. I love you. Come on, we go fishing, huh?

ELIAS *nods silently like a child.*

Come on.

BURKE *leads* ELIAS *out.* ELIZABETH *sings.*

Like A Rolling Stone

> Once upon a time you dressed so fine
> You threw the bums a dime in your prime, didn't you?
> People'd call, say, "Beware doll, you're bound to fall"
> You thought they were all kiddin' you
> You used to laugh about
> Everybody that was hangin' out
> Now you don't talk so loud
> Now you don't seem so proud
> About having to be scrounging for your next meal
>
> How does it feel
> How does it feel
> To be without a home
> Like a complete unknown
> Like a rolling stone?

You've gone to the finest school all right, Miss Lonely
But you know you only used to get juiced in it
And nobody has ever taught you how to live on the street
And now you find out you're gonna have to get used to it
You said you'd never compromise
With the mystery tramp, but now you realize
He's not selling any alibis
As you stare into the vacuum of his eyes
And ask him do you want to make a deal?

How does it feel
How does it feel
To be on your own
With no direction home
Like a complete unknown
Like a rolling stone?

We are in night-time. ELIZABETH *is at the radio. The music is now only in the radio.* MARIANNE *is making the room right for morning.*

SCOTT. How far are you along?

She looks at him. Looks away.

MARIANNE. Four and a half months. Say five.

SCOTT. Where's the daddy?

MARIANNE. Working the boats.

SCOTT. You gonna get married?

She shakes her head.

It's not too late to… I mean… You don't have to have it.

MARIANNE. At five months?

SCOTT. Depends who you ask. Where you go.

MARIANNE. No.

SCOTT (*weighs the situation up*). You raise it. Someone else raise it.

He turns away, dropping the subject.

MARIANNE. When you going to Chicago?

SCOTT. Tomorrow. Day after. Soon as I get me some dough. You do a deal with the pier man. He'll find you somewhere on board. You just stay out of the way. It's alright.

MARIANNE. You think I'd like Chicago, huh?

SCOTT. Chicago rises up off the plain like a magical kingdom when you see it first, I swear. And then… well, you go inside and they'll rob you kill you if you don't mind your business. But stay with someone who knows what they're doing? Then it's all just fine. I'll show you who to ask down on the pier, you want to go.

Pause.

You think about it. You let me know.

MARIANNE. Are you married, Mr Scott?

SCOTT. Yes I am. I got me a wife and two children. But I ain't seen 'em for a long time. My wife is with another man. I don't want to cause 'em all no trouble.

He hides his pain around this issue, but MARIANNE *has seen it.*

MARIANNE. Alright. Goodnight.

SCOTT. Goodnight.

MARIANNE. You know, you wouldn't believe me if I told you the truth.

SCOTT. About what?

MARIANNE. About my baby.

SCOTT. You don't have to tell me a damn thing.

She's taken aback. She stands there for a moment.

NICK *comes in. He senses the intimacy between* SCOTT *and* MARIANNE.

NICK. Watcha doin'?

MARIANNE. Cleaning up.

NICK. Get your momma some supper.

MARIANNE. Come on, Momma.

ELIZABETH. We going to the movies?

MARIANNE. Sure.

> NICK *looks at* SCOTT.

NICK. You okay?

SCOTT. Yes, sir.

NICK. Ha?

SCOTT (*his back to* NICK, *ignoring the bad vibe*). I'm fine.

NICK. Alright.

> SCOTT *goes.*

> (*To* MARIANNE.) You speak with Mr Perry last night?

> MARIANNE *continues her work, coming in and out of the kitchen.*

> You know he came all the way up here for that talk.

> MARIANNE *does her best to stay out of it.*

> You talk with him?

MARIANNE. Sure.

NICK. What did he say? He say anything?

MARIANNE. Sure.

NICK. Well that's… Did you… what did you…

MARIANNE. Nothin'.

NICK. Nothin'. What do you mean, nothin'? He brought you up them nice flowers, you didn't say nothing to him?

MARIANNE. Were those flowers for me?

NICK. Yeah!

MARIANNE. Well he took 'em with him.

NICK. What you mean?

MARIANNE. If they were for me he never said. He took them with him.

NICK. Well that's… Were you civil to him?

MARIANNE (*affronted*). What do you think I am?

NICK. That's a question! I'm not sure I rightly know! Stand still for one second. What you discuss? You didn't discuss nothing?

MARIANNE. Looks like all the discussin's already been done.

NICK. What are you talkin' about?

MARIANNE. He told me you and him already got it all planned out.

NICK. We may have… spoken. I may have answered some… I spoke with him, but it's… No one is saying you ain't got to want this for yourself.

MARIANNE. What could possibly make you think this is something I want? What you want make me go for?!

NICK. We *all* gotta go. It's just a question how we do it. When I went back down to Bakersfield for my uncle's funeral? All along the road? People living in tents. In tents! In the United States of America! Kids with no clothes on. All along the whole street into the town. There ain't no net to catch us, Marianne. You get it? You get it?

MARIANNE. Why don't you let me help you?

NICK. When I needed your help was when I needed you to be a good girl. That was when you coulda helped me.

MARIANNE. Daddy, I didn't…

NICK. Don't give me that cock-and-bull story. You gotta go carrying on with some goddamn boatman?! Like some little whore?!

MRS NEILSEN *has come through*.

MARIANNE *goes up through the kitchen*.

You okay?

MRS NEILSEN *smiles and nods.*

What you wanna waste your life away in here for?

MRS NEILSEN. I gotta waste it somewhere.

NICK *can't help smiling. He comes to* MRS NEILSEN *and takes her hand.*

ELIZABETH *is singing…*

Like A Rolling Stone

How does it feel
How does it feel
To be on your own
With no direction home

The band coming in softly underneath her. Over this the rest of the cast are harmonizing with…

I Want You

I want you
I want you
I want you
So bad
Honey I want you…

MARIANNE *comes on to the landing. Seeing* NICK, *she stops. They stand looking at each other for a moment.*

Black.

ACT TWO

The company sings.

You Ain't Goin' Nowhere

Clouds so swift
Rain won't lift
Gate won't close
Railings froze
Get your mind off wintertime
You ain't goin' nowhere
Whoo-ee! Ride me high
Tomorrow's the day
My bride's gonna come
Oh, oh, are we gonna fly
Down in the easy chair!

I don't care
How many letters they sent
Morning came and morning went
Pick up your money
And pack up your tent
You ain't goin' nowhere
Whoo-ee! Ride me high
Tomorrow's the day
My bride's gonna come
Oh, oh, are we gonna fly
Down in the easy chair!

Buy me a flute
And a gun that shoots
Tailgates and substitutes
Strap yourself
To the tree with roots
You ain't goin' nowhere

Whoo-ee! Ride me high
Tomorrow's the day
My bride's gonna come
Oh, oh, are we gonna fly
Down in the easy chair!

Genghis Khan
He could not keep
All his kings
Supplied with sleep
We'll climb that hill no matter how steep
When we get up to it
Whoo-ee! Ride me high
Tomorrow's the day
My bride's gonna come
Oh, oh, are we gonna fly
Down in the easy chair!

It segues into 'Jokerman'.

Jokerman

Standing on the waters casting your bread
While the eyes of the idol with the iron head are glowing
Distant ships sailing into the mist
You were born with a snake in both of your fists while a
    hurricane was blowing
Freedom just around the corner for you
But with the truth so far off, what good will it do?

Jokerman dance to the nightingale tune
Bird fly high by the light of the moon
Oh, oh, oh, Jokerman

*Some shadowy figures are upstage in the lamplight, maybe
singing or dancing or talking.* ELIZABETH *is dancing with*
ELIAS. *Further downstage,* MR BURKE *is drinking and
playing cards with* MRS NEILSEN.

Furthest downstage, DR WALKER *is dancing with* MRS
BURKE. *He addresses us.*

DR WALKER. Today is Wednesday November 21st 1934. The night before Thanksgiving. The last one we ever celebrated together.

MRS BURKE. You got any more drops?

He gives her a little bottle, she takes some.

DR WALKER. Keep it.

MRS BURKE. You sure?

DR WALKER. Six drops a day maximum.

MRS BURKE. Thank you.

DR WALKER. You don't want to become addicted.

MRS BURKE. Why not?

He looks at her.

It's something to do, isn't it? I'm kidding! Of course not. Six drops. You must have a nice house, Doctor.

DR WALKER. I have a nice house, but I only live in two rooms. I eat in one I sleep in the other.

MRS BURKE. We had a house bigger than this one, you know.

DR WALKER. I'm sure you did.

MRS BURKE. How would it be, do you think, if I came to your house some day?

He looks at her.

I only say this for talk.

DR WALKER. Well I'm sure that would be very pleasant.

MRS BURKE. You think? I think it would be really sad. If we coupled, I mean. We'd be like two lonely beasts in the field. And yet...

DR WALKER. Yes.

ELIZABETH. Yes!

They laugh.

MRS BURKE *is attending to* ELIAS.

DR WALKER. This time of year, a lost soul could always find a welcome up here. Suicide had increased by nearly one hundred per cent in the years after the crash. Single men led the way, followed closely by divorced women. My own marriage had failed in the years before. I say it failed, but really I failed. Failed to spark my wife's interest for very long. I saw her with the man she left me for one night. They were standing by the rail down on Michigan Street looking out on the water. And boy could he make her laugh. I'd never seen her eyes light up like that. Never seen them hide such dark promise. A little morphine helped. You just glide on by. You got your little secret trick. Then it turns and you realize it's got teeth and boy are they buried in your flesh. I weaned myself off of it.

ELIZABETH. Mostly.

DR WALKER. Mostly.

MR BURKE *lurches downstage towards* DR WALKER, *taking his glass of bourbon with him.*

MR BURKE. Hey, Doc! I heard your good buddy on the wireless this evening!

DR WALKER. I thought you might!

DR WALKER *is preparing an injection for* ELIZABETH.

MR BURKE. You do know what it is we really need, dontcha? In the White House? A strong man.

MRS NEILSEN (*finishing out the game, flipping cards into little piles, calling over to them*). Bullcrap. What we need is a good man.

MR BURKE. Good, bad, I'm sick a hearing 'FDR is a good man' this and 'FDR is a good man' that.

He playfully tussles with and cuddles ELIAS.

DR WALKER (*laughs*). Sorry to hear that, Frank.

MR BURKE. I couldn't care less if he's yay or nay or rollin' in the hay. Long as the head man is strong I don't care two sausages if he's any good. 'Cause what we need is energy.

ELIZABETH. Energy!

MR BURKE. That's right, Mrs Laine! Energy – not morals!!

ELIZABETH. Woo-hoo!!

MRS NEILSEN *follows* MR BURKE *and takes his cards from his hand.*

MRS NEILSEN. That's actually my trick!

MR BURKE. Oh sorry yes. That's what I meant. Here you go.

MRS NEILSEN. Thank you. You want another game? Double or nothing?

MR BURKE. No – Jesus! Energy!

ELIZABETH. Energy!

MR BURKE. You know. Just someone doin' something – even if it's the wrong thing – somethin's happenin'. And when somethin's happenin', somethin' else happens. Then, 'cause a that – something else happens. People start gettin' ideas. Start feelin' like they can do somethin' about it. Put what they know to good use.

MRS NEILSEN *pours herself a drink.*

MRS NEILSEN. Huh. Yeah. You know, people say they're can't be no more wars now 'cause we all know it's no good. We don't know shit if you ask me. Excuse my language.

MR BURKE. I like your language.

MRS NEILSEN. Everybody gotta make their *own* mistakes and anyone thinks we don't is a fuckin' banana if you ask me.

MR BURKE (*points at her*). That's beautifully put.

MRS NEILSEN (*deadpan*). You like that?

MR BURKE. 'Anyone who thinks we won't is a fuckin' banana.'

MRS BURKE (*to* MR BURKE). You're a fuckin' banana.

She spots NICK *coming through to talk with* DR WALKER.

Nick.

NICK. How are you this evening, Mrs Burke?

MRS BURKE (*straight in, privately*). Nick, I have to ask you if
we can extend our credit.

NICK. Extend it in which direction?

MRS BURKE. Francis has an old partner down in Rush City
who has six hundred dollars he's been waiting to pay him.
It's just a question of the weather, you see. It's tricky getting
down there.

NICK. The weather, huh? When do you think it's gonna…

MRS BURKE. Nick. I know we owe you.

NICK. It's alright.

MRS BURKE *suddenly puts her face in her hands, hiding
her tears.*

Come on now.

NICK *puts an arm round her.*

MRS BURKE (*a rush of words*). If my mother saw me here
now, she'd die. She'd be so ashamed. She'd hate to feel so
helpless to help me. Is your mother still alive, Nick?

NICK. I hope not.

MRS BURKE. Why?

NICK. 'Cause we buried her beside my dad end of 1929.

MRS BURKE *can't help laughing.*

You still got your dignity, Mrs Burke.

MRS BURKE. Thank you, Nick.

NICK. You just help yourself to a pop a bourbon in there – you
know my little stash. You listen to the wireless. It's alright
tonight. Everything's just fine tonight.

MRS BURKE *gets herself together and goes back to the
others.*

NICK *is with* DR WALKER *and* ELIZABETH.
DR WALKER *looks into her eyes with a handheld
ophthalmoscope. She seems unresponsive. He stands holding*

her hand looking at her. NICK *pours himself a cup of coffee.*
Stands watching DR WALKER*'s careful, gentle treatment of*
ELIZABETH. *She is smiling at* DR WALKER.

Latest is she says she hears stuff?

DR WALKER. Hears what?

NICK. A girl down a hole.

DR WALKER. Okay.

NICK. I know who it is. That's the… That's the… [crazy thing.]

DR WALKER. You were a kid, Nick. You were just a kid.

NICK *shrugs.*

You'd… come and see me, wouldn't you, Nick? I mean… if
something was really bothering you, right?

NICK. Sure! If there was something you could do about it. You
write me a prescription for thirty thousand dollars I'll be
right as rain.

DR WALKER *laughs and gets up to go. He watches*
MARIANNE *dancing with* SCOTT *upstage. He turns*
to NICK.

DR WALKER. Nick – You know what pseudocyesis is?

NICK. Pseudo-what?

DR WALKER. Cyesis.

NICK. What is it?

DR WALKER. Well, sometimes if a girl feels an intense need
to… connect to something or to… well, to have a baby. Her
body can manifest all the signs of a real pregnancy.
Menstrual cycle stops, belly swells up, morning sickness, she
might even feel the baby moving… these symptoms can be
very convincing, Nick.

NICK. What are you saying this to me for?

Just then, PERRY *comes in, holding his bunch of flowers.*

PERRY. Dr Walker.

DR WALKER. Mr Perry. Right, well, I'll…

DR WALKER *leaves, goes through to the other room.*

NICK. What.

PERRY. I didn't say anything.

NICK. What.

PERRY. Nothing.

NICK. I can feel it. What.

PERRY. No, I…

NICK. Yeah?

PERRY. I just feel like I'm… It's almost like I'm getting to where you're making me beg.

NICK. Beg?

PERRY. Yet I'm the one doing *you* a favor!

NICK. I'm not asking you to do a damn thing. What do you want me to do?

PERRY. Maybe ask her to come down to my store, will ya?

NICK. She won't go down to your store.

PERRY. Then what am I doing here?

PERRY *starts to go,* NICK *stops him.*

NICK. No, wait, wait, wait. We got a plan here.

PERRY. What's the plan?

NICK. Well for starters – don't beg!

PERRY. So what am I…?

NICK. You just say. You just say, 'Let's go and talk and…'

PERRY. We've talked. I've talked to her.

NICK. Talk to her again. Lay it out.

PERRY. You lay it out.

NICK. I've laid it out! Now you lay it out! You give me two thousand dollars, help me put a new roof on this place. New floors. New windows. New walls. Show the bank what this can be. You realize the revenue's gonna flow outta here? We just need to – (*Joins his fingers up to demonstrate their deal coming together.*)

PERRY. Jesus. What the fuck is happening to me? How do we ever think any of the crazy shit we do is a good idea? I mean, how does that happen? Who's pulling the strings?

ELIZABETH (*suddenly lucid*). Then find someone your own age. You old goat.

PERRY (*rounds on her angrily*). You don't think I've tried? You don't think I want that? How do you do it? Where do you go? I talk to women who come in my store – in that way – what would people say?

NICK. Just be friendly.

PERRY. I'm friendly. I'm friendly, Nick. People just take it the wrong way!

NICK. That's why this gives you an advantage.

PERRY. How?

NICK. 'Cause you're *helping* her. You're helping *me*. Feel good, Mr Perry. For God's sake. Feel good! This is good! You think I just called in by your store on some whim? What do you think I am? Some dumb idiot?

PERRY *looks at* NICK, *but doesn't answer that one.*

PERRY. May I use your water closet?

NICK. My what?

PERRY. Water closet.

NICK. Oh sure. Right around there. Through the kitchen.

PERRY. Thank you. You know what? I'm… gonna go for a walk.

NICK. Good idea. Go get a drink. Go get a milkshake. Come back. Alright? Stop worrying! Will ya?

NICK *goes to him awkwardly as though unsure whether to embrace him or not. He ends up putting one arm round* PERRY. PERRY *isn't sure what is happening.* NICK *laughs pathetically.* PERRY *goes out, bringing his flowers with him.*

ELIZABETH. Well, Nick.

NICK *ignores her.*

Well, Nick.

NICK. What.

ELIZABETH. Just well, Nick.

NICK (*not very interested*). Mm-hm?

ELIZABETH. You think I don't see? You think I don't *give* a good goddamn? You don't think I give a good wocky-woo?

NICK. Elizabeth, I don't know what you give or what you get.

ELIZABETH. Yeah, whadya whadya whadya whadya whadya.

NICK. What.

ELIZABETH. Shut up.

NICK. You have to be rude?

ELIZABETH. You think this is rude? You ain't seen rude. You think I care? Huh? About your little lady woman up in your attic. (*As though talking to a child, patronisingly.*) It's alright, Nicky Wicky. Animals got to feel the warm, right? I'mma not care one way or tother nother.

NICK. So what you so angry about then? You don't think I do enough? You don't think I couldn't get you put away in some old lady's home like that – (*Snaps fingers.*)

ELIZABETH. You're too mean.

NICK. They'd take you away. Nobody would say I haven't put up with enough fucking crap. Offa you. Offa everybody.

ELIZABETH. Oh boo boo boo, boo boo boo boo, poor boo.

NICK. Elizabeth, I swear to God I'll knock your damn teeth in.

ELIZABETH. Oh knock my deed in. You'll knock my deed in. How much money you get?

NICK. Money where?

ELIZABETH. Off a the money man. The shoe man.

NICK. What money?

ELIZABETH. Whatcha have to stick her in his old dirty bed for?

NICK. Girl needs help. Whatcha want? You want her goin' round
the roads? Dragging her baby? Tramping in the dirt? I ain't got
nothin for her.

ELIZABETH. Be like sleeping in a damn grave – his cold feet
like clay comin' round her. At least in a whorehouse she can
name her own price.

NICK suddenly grabs ELIZABETH, *shaking her. She fights
back as they argue.*

NICK. What happened to you? Where's my wife? Where's my
damn wife?

ELIZABETH. Devil took her bitch.

NICK. Well that'd explain it! You're crazier than a ship's rat but
you were never stupid, Elizabeth. You know. I don't find that
money, the banker gonna take everything. We'll be like dust
in the wind here! I gotta make these decisions. I gotta make
'em on my own!

ELIZABETH *practices some dance steps.*

ELIZABETH. You'll find the money.

NICK. Where?!

ELIZABETH. Find it off a your old-assed girlfriend. Let her
figure it out.

NICK *can't help laughing. He softens towards her.*

NICK. You want a coffee?

*He touches her, maybe even kisses her on the forehead. But
she has gone somewhere inside herself.*

ELIZABETH. You hear the girl down the hole?

NICK. What?

ELIZABETH. I know you hear it.

NICK. Why don't you shut your fucking mouth?

ELIZABETH. I know you do. You hear it more than me!

NICK suddenly grabs ELIZABETH. *She fights him.*

You do! You do! You do!

NICK. I don't hear nothing! I don't hear a damn thing! Shut up! You hear me? You shut up!

ELIZABETH *pulls away, she puts her hands to her face.* NICK *stands there looking helplessly at her.*

I'm sorry. Elizabeth. I'm sorry alright?

He goes to her. He takes her in his arms, picks her up and carries her to bed. A performance of 'Sweetheart Like You': while he dresses her, MRS NEILSON *coming to help.* MRS BURKE *and* MRS NEILSEN *sing.*

Sweetheart Like You

> Well, the pressure's down, the boss ain't here
> He gone North, he ain't around
> They say that vanity got the best of him
> But he sure left here after sundown
> By the way, that's a cute hat
> And that smile's so hard to resist
> But what's a sweetheart like you doin' in a dump like this?
>
> You know, I once knew a woman who looked like you
> She wanted a whole man, not just a half
> She used to call me sweet daddy when I was only a child
> You kind of remind me of her when you laugh
> In order to deal in this game, got to make the queen
>   disappear
> It's done with a flick of the wrist
> What's a sweetheart like you doin' in a dump like this?
>
> …
>
> You know you can make a name for yourself
> You can hear them tires squeal

You can be known as the most beautiful woman
Who ever crawled across cut glass to make a deal

A smack of the snare drum and MRS NEILSEN *soars into* –

True Love Tends To Forget

I'm getting weary looking in my baby's eyes
When she's near me she's so hard to recognize
I finally realize there's no room for regret
True love, true love, true love tends to forget

Hold me, baby be near
You told me that you'd be sincere
Every day of the year's like playin' Russian roulette
True love, true love, true love tends to forget

I was lyin' down in the reeds without any oxygen
I saw you in the wilderness among the men
Saw you drift into infinity and come back again
All you got to do is wait and I'll tell you when

Underscore…

MRS NEILSEN. I'm gonna go, Nick. I can't pay you no more.

NICK. What are you talking about?

MRS NEILSEN. I went to see Mr St Clair about signing all
the forms.

NICK. When?

MRS NEILSEN. Today.

NICK. Yeah?

MRS NEILSEN. Turns out I owe him money.

NICK. You'll pay him when you get your inheritance.

MRS NEILSEN. The legal fees ate it all up! There ain't nothing
for me or anyone else.

NICK. You're kidding me.

MRS NEILSEN *shakes her head.*

That goddamn crook! I'm gonna go down there myself and I'll…

MRS NEILSEN. He showed me the figures, Nick. It was all there in black and white.

NICK (*floored*). You're kidding me…

NICK *exhales, unable to hide his feelings. He gets up and goes to look out the window.*

MRS NEILSEN. I know you need the room. I'll clear out.

NICK. What?! Where?

MRS NEILSEN. My sister.

NICK. In Minneapolis?

MRS NEILSEN. No, my twin sister. In Oklahoma.

NICK. Oklahoma?! Are you nuts?!

MRS NEILSEN. Oklahoma City. She's married to a schoolteacher.

NICK (*sarcastic*). Oh! Right!

MRS NEILSEN. She can put me up for a while.

NICK (*exasperated*). Right.

MRS NEILSEN. Maybe find me some work out there.

NICK. Yeah.

MRS NEILSEN. We ain't gonna buy no hotel, Nick.

NICK. Huh. It's all over I guess.

MRS NEILSEN. Don't speak like that. Do you love me?

NICK. What?

MRS NEILSEN. Can you love me?

NICK. What kind of question is that?

MRS NEILSEN. I can take it either way. But you gotta tell me the truth.

NICK. You just said it's all bullshit!

MRS NEILSEN. Yeah it's all bullshit. It's still all I got!

NICK. We ain't spring chickens.

MRS NEILSEN. What's that gotta do with it?

NICK. You live too long, you see too much. It chips away at you. How can you love someone who ain't got a soul?

MRS NEILSEN. You have a soul.

NICK. I don't feel it.

MRS NEILSEN. I feel it. Just say it to me. Just say it.

NICK. I can't love anyone! There it is! There's the truth!

MRS NEILSEN. Can't or won't?

He can't answer her. Can't look at her. She sings.

True Love Tends To Forget

> I was lyin' down in the reeds without any oxygen
> I saw you in the wilderness among the men
> Saw you drift into infinity and come back again
> All you got to do is wait and I'll tell you when
>
> You belong to me, baby, without any doubt
> Don't forsake me, baby, don't sell me out
> Don't keep me knockin' about from Mexico to Tibet
> True love, true love, true love tends to forget

Spoken or sung words from 'Sweetheart Like You', along with the music:

Sweetheart Like You

> They say that patriotism is the last refuge
> To which a scoundrel clings
> Steal a little and they throw you in jail
> Steal a lot and they make you king
> There's only one step down from here, baby
> It's called the land of permanent bliss
> What's a sweetheart like you doin' in a dump like this?

It's morning. NICK *comes out on the porch.* PERRY *has returned with his wilted-looking flowers.*

PERRY. Happy Thanksgiving, Nick.

NICK (*startled*). Jesus Christ! Yeah – Happy Thanksgiving, Mr Perry. (*Sotto.*) You been out here all night? Look at you, you're freezing! Get inside.

NICK *drags him inside.* PERRY *meets* ELIZABETH *in the hallway.*

PERRY. Happy Thanksgiving, Elizabeth.

NICK. Get in here.

MARIANNE *is fixing up the room for a big Thanksgiving meal.* NICK *shoves* PERRY *in.*

Well look who's here!! Let me, eh… Let me just…

He nods aggressively to PERRY *and leaves.* NICK *tries to take* ELIZABETH *with him, but she slips back in, watching* PERRY.

PERRY. Well, Happy Thanksgiving, Marianne!

MARIANNE. Happy Thanksgiving, Mr Perry.

PERRY. How are you?

MARIANNE. Pretty much as well as I was when you saw me yesterday.

PERRY. I can worry about you, can't I?

MARIANNE. I guess. But you don't know me all that much.

PERRY. Would you believe me if I said I feel I do know you?

MARIANNE. How?

PERRY. I guess God's goodness shines down and it makes things happen. Things you couldn't dream of I guess.

ELIZABETH. I guess.

MARIANNE. Mmm.

MARIANNE *goes to the piano and plays while they converse.*

PERRY. Maybe my whole life has been leading me right here to give you and your child shelter. Who can say? (*Laughs pathetically.*) I mean, that makes about as much sense as anything else as far as I can make out!

MARIANNE. Maybe you're just a predator.

PERRY. A predator.

MARIANNE. Sure.

PERRY. I don't think so.

MARIANNE. Well how would you know?

PERRY. I think I'd know if I was a predator, Marianne.

MARIANNE. Maybe you wouldn't. Maybe you have to believe you're going round doing good deeds so as to enable you to go on the hunt. You know, on the prowl.

PERRY. I don't think so.

MARIANNE. No, huh? My pa didn't say nothing about all the trouble we had here?

PERRY. Trouble is everywhere. I know.

MARIANNE. I'm talking about troubles no one can explain.

PERRY. Explain what?

MARIANNE. That night. The night I… the night the wind came in my room. I woke up. All I knew then was… someone was there.

PERRY. A man came in your room?

MARIANNE. It was deeper than a man. Older than a man. When I pressed my face into his tunic and I breathed in, I could smell, like, ancient water. You know that smell like water under the ground? Like stone? And when I breathed in more and more it was like I was breathing through him. And I could see through him – into the ancient past. A figure in a boat, and someone was singing and I… That's how it happened.

PERRY. Marianne, however it happened, you got yourself in trouble. All your daddy wants is to look at our options here.

MARIANNE. You look like a weak man, Mr Perry. But you got some steel buried in there keeps you cutting in the woods.

PERRY *suddenly confronts* MARIANNE *aggressively*.

Out in the kitchen a girl sings 'Girl From The North Country', other guests harmonizing.

PERRY. Hey! I don't need to come down here and be told I'm weak! You don't know what I been going through every day since your daddy came to me! What would you know about it? You haven't got a damned pot to piss in and you subject me to this? Let me tell you something. Your daddy can't take care a you. This house? It's gonna all be taken by the bank. Your daddy's old to work on a farm or a factory – even if there was work. Bottle's got your brother. Who knows where your mama's gone? Where you gonna go? A black girl with a black baby? You want me to tell you? You're gonna be made to give that baby away and then you can whistle your way down to St Louis or somewhere work as a maid. That's all you are. Now you and me both got a chance. My wife came and told me in a dream, Marianne. My wife!! You just get in under my roof, girl, and I won't never touch you, that's a promise. Nobody chooses to get old. Everybody fights it. But it kicks your ass. You can't win. You move slower and slower 'cause you can't go fast! It hurts! Pain's got ya surrounded.

Your back and your legs and your hands in here in your gut?! You wake in the night, there's no one there. Only the cold. And one way down. You remember a warm light and a smile from long ago. But doesn't help. It only hurts.

Something in his tone has landed deep inside her. She stands looking at him in silence. NICK *returns*.

NICK. So we doin'? Huh?

MARIANNE *looks at* NICK.

ELIZABETH. Oh he's just been showing everybody his Vienna sausage.

NICK *ignores her*.

PERRY. Give me a date and I'll write you a cheque.

NICK. How about Christmas Eve?

PERRY *nods*. NICK *shakes his hand*.

Stay for lunch.

PERRY *nods*.

ELIZABETH *is playing the piano – 'Ballad Of A Thin Man'. MARIANNE continues her work.* MRS BURKE *and other guests are setting up a Thanksgiving dinner.*

GENE *comes through*.

GENE. Happy Thanksgiving.

NICK. What you doing? Gettin' up or goin' to bed?

GENE. Getting up.

NICK. At four thirty?

GENE. If it's four thirty then, yeah.

GENE *is putting fancy shoes on* ELIZABETH'*s feet*.

NICK. You go down to that eh…

GENE. Sure.

NICK. Well?

GENE. Yeah.

NICK. Yeah?

GENE. Yeah it's…

NICK. We're talking about the interview?

GENE. Yeah, I know.

NICK. And?

GENE. Yeah.

NICK. It's all good?

GENE. All good. He said the railroad's gonna lift all the boats round here. Bright guy like me, start in the office, working my way up…

NICK. That's right…

GENE. Said it was just what they wanted to see.

NICK. Didn't I tell you?

GENE. Yeah.

NICK. Huh?

GENE. Yeah.

NICK. Gene…

    NICK *shakes* GENE*'s hand.*

    You're a good boy.

    GENE *nods, goes on his way.* NICK *goes down into the kitchen.*

    DR WALKER *is in the dining room with the guests.*

    MRS BURKE *is dancing with* SCOTT *to the music someone plays on the piano. The guests are drinking wine.* ELIZABETH *dances with* MRS NEILSEN. PERRY *drinks a cup of coffee.*

    Someone starts strumming a ukulele – the infectious opening chords of 'Hurricane'. The double bass takes the walking bass line and someone scratches a wild fiddle over it. SCOTT *sings.*

Hurricane

    Pistol shots ring out in the barroom night
    Enter Patty Valentine from the upper hall
    She sees the bartender in a pool of blood
    Cries out, 'My God, they killed them all!'
    Here comes the story of the Hurricane
    The man the authorities came to blame
    For somethin' that he never done
    Put in a prison cell, but one time he could-a been
    The champion of the world

    Three bodies lyin' there does Patty see
    And another man named Bello, movin' around
       mysteriously

'I didn't do it,' he says, and he throws up his hands
'I was only robbin' the register, I hope you understand
I saw them leavin',' he says, and he stops
'One of us had better call up the cops'
And so Patty calls the cops
And they arrive on the scene with their red lights flashin'
In the hot New Jersey night

Meanwhile, far away in another part of town
Rubin Carter and a couple of friends are drivin' around
Number one contender for the middleweight crown
Had no idea what kinda shit was about to go down
When a cop pulled him over to the side of the road
Just like the time before and the time before that
In Paterson that's just the way things go
If you're black you might as well not show up on the
    street
'Less you wanna draw the heat

Segue to 'Idiot Wind'. MARIANNE *and* SCOTT *sing.*

Idiot Wind

Someone's got it in for me, they're planting stories in
    the press
Whoever it is I wish they'd cut it out but when they will
    I can only guess
They say I shot a man named Gray and took his wife
    to Italy
She inherited a million bucks and when she died it came
    to me
I can't help it if I'm lucky

…

Idiot wind, blowing every time you move your mouth
Blowing down the backroads headin' south
Idiot wind, blowing every time you move your teeth
You're an idiot, babe
It's a wonder that you still know how to breathe

…

Idiot wind, blowing through the flowers on your tomb
Blowing through the curtains in your room
Idiot wind, blowing every time you move your teeth
You're an idiot, babe
It's a wonder that you still know how to breathe

It was gravity which pulled us down and destiny which
    broke us apart
You tamed the lion in my cage but it just wasn't enough to
    change my heart
Now everything's a little upside down, as a matter of fact
    the wheels have stopped
What's good is bad, what's bad is good, you'll find out
    when you reach the top
You're on the bottom

   …

Idiot wind, blowing through the buttons of our coats
Blowing through the letters that we wrote
Idiot wind, blowing through the dust upon our shelves
We're idiots, babe
It's a wonder we can even feed ourselves

The guests all enjoy dancing around. The music softens, the fiddle playing softly against the uke…

MRS BURKE. Happy Thanksgiving, Nick!

NICK. Happy Thanksgiving, Mrs Burke, Mr Scott.

SCOTT. Same to you, sir.

    MARIANNE *comes to* GENE. *She takes his hand and they dance.*

MRS BURKE. Where's Elias?

MR BURKE. We had a walk. He's sleeping.

    NICK *comes through with fuel for the stove.*

    Well look at all this! Happy Thanksgiving, Nick!

NICK. To you too – Marianne cooked the turkey, so…

MR BURKE. Marianne, you are a genius.

MARIANNE. I wouldn't say that. You can make yourself a sandwich – cranberry's all in the bowl.

MR BURKE. Holy shamoly.

NICK. We always do a sandwich. Then you don't have to do all that – you know – sitting at the same table, right?

MR BURKE. Yeah – everybody looking at each other! I get it. I'm the king of the sandwiches.

MR BURKE *stumbles a little drunkenly.*

MRS NEILSEN. Here, let me make you one.

MR BURKE. I always liked you, Mrs Neilsen, you have a way about you. Doesn't she have a way about her?

MRS NEILSEN. What kind of a way?!

MR BURKE. A way! A way! Nick knows! Right? Am I right?

MRS BURKE. Ignore him, Mrs Neilsen. You think Elias wants a sandwich?

MR BURKE. Leave him, he's sleeping. (*To* MRS NEILSEN.) I dunno what it is – it's the confluence between your eyes and your eyebrows. Somehow they suggest a gateway to the eternal.

MRS NEILSEN. I'm just making you a sandwich!

MRS BURKE. What in God's name are you talking about?

MR BURKE. You look out, Joe, she's got them talons, once they get into you, you'll never get away.

SCOTT. I don't know about that, but she can dance.

MRS BURKE. You mind not talking about me like I'm not here?

SCOTT. I'm sorry, excuse me.

MR BURKE. It's only good things! We're only saying nice things! You look out. How many drinks has she had?

MRS BURKE. Not as many as you clearly. (*To* SCOTT.) I never felt arms like these.

SCOTT. Thank you, ma'am.

MRS BURKE. I mean it – you ever feel arms like that, Nick?

NICK. Not lately.

> *The live music in the room stops while people eat.* DR
> WALKER *puts on the wireless. A 1930s arrangement of
> 'Lay Down Your Weary Tune' is on.* MARIANNE *is near*
> DR WALKER.

DR WALKER. How are you, Marianne?

MARIANNE. Fine, thank you.

DR WALKER. You want to call by – next week?

MARIANNE. Sure.

DR WALKER. Unless you want to see someone else.

MARIANNE. No, that's fine.

MRS BURKE. Should I go get Elias? He's missing everything.

MR BURKE. Leave him alone.

> NICK *smiles at* MRS NEILSEN. *She doesn't give him one
> back. Embarrassed, he addresses the room.*

NICK. Anyone been outside? Man, it's cold.

DR WALKER. Sure is.

MR BURKE. Mmm! You see the snow?

DR WALKER. Mm-hm.

NICK. That's how it starts. Those dry flakes like that? That's
North Pole air. Sit down!

MR BURKE. I'm good. I like standing. It's like swaying around
on a ship.

> MR BURKE *and* NICK *watch the dancing for a few
> moments. Then* NICK *goes back to kitchen.* MRS BURKE
> *sees* MR BURKE *helping himself to a drink.*

MRS BURKE (*to* MR BURKE). You want to go easy?

MR BURKE (*calling in to* NICK). A sick child gets inside you
somehow, Nick.

NICK (*off*). What's that?

MR BURKE (*calling to* NICK). I guess you can't help it. It's down there underneath everything.

MARLOWE *comes in.*

MARLOWE. Happy Thanksgiving. Hello, all. What about that wind! It's like a knife!

MR BURKE. Reverend. The very fellow. Happy Thanksgiving. Have a sandwich. I was just saying. A sick child.

MARLOWE (*instant sympathy*). Oh, but of course.

MR BURKE. I mean, one moment there you are, in your life, kind of a child yourself.

NICK *comes back in, apron on, pouring some coffee for the guests.*

MRS BURKE. Oh where is he?

MRS BURKE *goes to find* ELIAS.

MR BURKE. You have responsibilities, you have worries, sure, but it's mostly about yourself, your intended, your wife, the few dollars in your pocket, the normal things. And you think when that baby comes along how complete things will be. What no one tells you is – Jesus Christ – a child is hard work, brother!

They laugh. MR BURKE *takes a cup offered to him, by* SCOTT. *He continues, jovially, warmly.*

For sure. Listen, I'm not saying I was there when it was hardest. I could escape to my office, find peace in my dreams and the hurly-burly and the fights and arguments which all men truly enjoy.

MRS BURKE *comes back through, looking for* ELIAS.

MRS BURKE. Where'd you say he was?

MR BURKE (*indicates vaguely*). He's…

MRS BURKE. You need to lie down. (*To* MARLOWE *and* NICK.) I apologize.

MRS BURKE *looks out the window and goes out through the kitchen.* GENE *and* SCOTT *are getting something to eat.*

MR BURKE. She'll tell you. I tried – to put in the hours. It's…
it's… I mean, it'll drive you crazy because a child is only
learning. They wanna do the most mundane little thing over
and over again – it's torture! If you're not in the mood, ha,
ha, ha – (*A qualifying little laugh.*) Thinking to yourself, it'll
get easier when he's older. But he never got any older!
(*Laughs.*)

NICK (*putting wood in the stove*). He's a good boy.

MR BURKE. Right! He just got bigger and bigger! The nights
I stood on the landing outside his door, listening to the
strange noises he made. Laura sitting inside in there with
him. I was… afraid to go in. I could face down eighty men
threatening to strike. Righteous anger, lifting me up in a
chariot of hatred, but a child's cries. A big grown child
crying in the night, why, it rips the floor from underneath
you. And then. In the crash. The money's gone. The business
is gone. They say they're coming for your house! And there
you are. You're naked. You have to just be a… a father.
That's all you are. That's all that's left. But you're a father to
this helpless… This creature. Full of strength and longings
and drives he doesn't understand. You turn your back on him
for one second and he gets out…

MRS BURKE *comes back.*

MRS BURKE. Francis…

MR BURKE. He gets out and you're frantically searching for
him all up and down in the neighbors' yards…

MRS BURKE. Francis…

MR BURKE. If the unthinkable happens… if he's done
something, to someone, it's… it's…

MRS BURKE. Francis…

MR BURKE. It's beyond a nightmare. 'Cause a nightmare ends.

MRS BURKE (*turning off the wireless*). Francis. Where's Elias?

MR BURKE. He's sleeping. I told you. We went for a walk is
all. Went for one of our long ones. Down for a look at the
water.

MRS BURKE. Where is he, Francis?

MR BURKE. I told you.

MRS BURKE. He's not here!

She goes out again. We hear her calling for ELIAS.

NICK. Where is he, Frank?

MR BURKE. The water was like iron.

NICK. Where is he?

MR BURKE. It was an accident. That's...

MRS BURKE *comes back*

MRS BURKE. Where is he?! Where is he?

MR BURKE. It was an accident. I couldn't stop it.

Silence.

NICK. Where is he, Frank?

MR BURKE. He's on the shore, Nick. He's asleep.

Silence.

MRS BURKE.... What?!

MARLOWE. Oh, Mrs Burke.

MR BURKE. Where's your God now, Reverend, huh?

MARLOWE. He's everywhere.

MR BURKE. That's right.

MRS BURKE. Are you all crazy? Are you all fucking crazy? He's a baby! Oh Mrs Neilsen! Mrs Neilsen!

NICK. Frank. What happened?

MR BURKE. The water was like iron.

MRS BURKE. You fuckin'... You fuckin'... You didn't even... (*Goes to* MR BURKE, *starts thumping him with her fists*.) You didn't even say nothin'. You never said a goddamn thing! You dirty bastard!

NICK *and* MRS NEILSEN *pull* MRS BURKE *off* MR
BURKE. *The band come through with* ELIAS*'s ghost, free of
pain, worry or limitations, singing.*

Duquesne Whistle

> Listen to that Duquesne whistle blowin'
> Blowin' like it's gonna sweep my world away
> I'm gonna stop in Carbondale and keep on going
> That Duquesne train gonna ride me night and day
>
> You say I'm a gambler, you say I'm a pimp
> But I ain't neither one
>
> Listen to that Duquesne whistle blowin'
> Sound like it's on a final run
>
> Listen to that Duquesne whistle blowin'
> Blowin' like she never blowed before
> Blue light blinkin', red light glowin'
> Blowin' like she's at my chamber door
>
> You smiling through the fence at me
> Just like you always smiled before
>
> Listen to that Duquesne whistle blowin'
> Blowin' like she ain't gonna blow no more
>
> Can't you hear that Duquesne whistle blowin'
> Blowin' like the sky's gonna blow apart
> You're the only thing alive that keeps me goin'
> You're like a time bomb in my heart
>
> I can hear a sweet voice gently calling
> Must be the Mother of our Lord
>
> Listen to that Duquesne whistle blowin'
> Blowin' like my woman's on board

And a sudden move into 'Señor (Tales Of Yankee Power)'.
ELIAS, KATE *and* MARLOWE *take the lead, singing.*

Señor (Tales Of Yankee Power)

Señor, señor, do you know where we're headin'?
Lincoln County Road or Armageddon?
Seems like I been down this way before
Is there any truth in that, señor?

Señor, señor, do you know where she is hidin'?
How long are we gonna be ridin'?
How long must I keep my eyes glued to the door?
Will there be any comfort there, señor?

There's a wicked wind still blowin' on that upper deck
There's an iron cross still hangin' down from around
    her neck
There's a marchin' band still playin' in that vacant lot
Where she held me in her arms one time and said, 'Forget
    me not'

…

Well, the last thing I remember before I stripped and
    kneeled
Was that trainload of fools bogged down in a magnetic
    field
A gypsy with a broken flag and a flashing ring
Said, 'Son, this ain't a dream no more, it's the real thing'

…

Señor, señor, let's disconnect these cables
Overturn these tables
This place don't make sense to me no more
Can you tell me what we're waiting for, señor?

Becoming: 'Is Your Love In Vain'. MR *and* MRS BURKE
sing.

Is Your Love In Vain?

Do you love me, or are you just extending goodwill?
Do you need me half as bad as you say, or are you just
    feeling guilt?

I've been burned before and I know the score
So you won't hear me complain
Will I be able to count on you
Or is your love in vain?

Are you so fast that you cannot see that I must have
    solitude?
When I am in the darkness, why do you intrude?
Do you know my world, do you know my kind
Or must I explain?
Will you let me be myself
Or is your love in vain?

Well I've been to the mountain and I've been in the wind
I've been in and out of happiness
I have dined with kings, I've been offered wings
And I've never been too impressed

All right, I'll take a chance, I will fall in love with you
If I'm a fool you can have the night, you can have the
    morning too
Can you cook and sew, make flowers grow
Do you understand my pain?
Are you willing to risk it all
Or is your love in vain?

Evening. MARIANNE *is alone with* SCOTT. *Outside the storm is blowing hard. She glances at him, but continues with her work, going in and out of the kitchen. He hangs around the kitchen. Underscore for 'The Times They Are A-Changin'' and 'Hurricane' play beneath their scene…*

SCOTT. You given any more thought to what I said?

She doesn't answer.

You hear that storm? I gotta be on that boat leaves at ten o'clock. Else nobody'll be going anywhere. (*Pause.*) You gonna dignify me with an answer?

MARIANNE. What do you care where I go?

SCOTT. I don't know! Just feels like I gotta take you.

MARIANNE. And I just gotta go along?

SCOTT. I know you don't know me. I know it's crazy. But there's crazier things happened in this house far as I can see.

MARIANNE. This is a bad time, Mr Scott.

SCOTT. It's always bad times!

MARIANNE. You know, they say some coloreds tried to rob a store in town last night.

SCOTT. I don't know a damn thing about that.

MARIANNE. No, huh?

SCOTT. I just told you. What am I? The only colored you ever seen?

MARIANNE. You're the only one I ever saw says he's no money, next day he's all for jumping on a boat – take along a woman he only just met.

SCOTT. I'm tryna do you a good turn, you wanna whip round, put this crap in my face?

MARIANNE *turns away.* SCOTT *follows her into the dining room.*

Don't you walk away from me. Don't you walk away from me like that. If we're gonna go that road together, even for a short while, you best be able to look me in the eyes and know what I am. At least gimme that. I ain't got nothing else in it taking you on.

MARIANNE. No, huh? I ain't stupid.

SCOTT. I never said you was.

MARIANNE. I can read a paper.

SCOTT. So what?

MARIANNE. I see two convicts escaped outta Peytonville a week ago. Who's the other one? That preacher?

SCOTT. Maybe I ain't never been no savior, but I ain't never killed no one either! And if I'm walking the streets right now when some judge says I gotta rot my life away in some rat hole, well maybe he's wrong! You think I'm the only nigger was in the joint serving somebody else's stretch? You look in my eyes and if you don't believe me, that's alright. I'll go. But if you can see me… I'm saying, if you can see me…

ELIZABETH *comes in. The underscore ends…*

You want to come down to Chicago, you meet me at the coffee house on the corner at eight thirty. You're not there I'll… Yeah.

SCOTT *goes out.*

ELIZABETH. Fix me, will you? Fix me. (*Indicates her clothes and hair.*) I'm such a goddamn mess! What happened?

MARIANNE *starts to fix* ELIZABETH *up.*

MARIANNE. Mama. I'm going away.

ELIZABETH. You're not going away. You're not going away. You just got here.

MARIANNE. Mama… (*Comes to* ELIZABETH, *burying her head in her shoulder.*)

ELIZABETH. Shhh. That's alright. That's alright. Just don't play with knives. You know the Devil's only tryna be your friend 'cause you give him your blood.

MARIANNE *nods silently.* ELIZABETH *sings a few lines of a lullaby, but it feels strange rather than comforting.*

MARLOWE *comes in looking for food.*

MARLOWE. Evening…

ELIZABETH. Here he is, the word of the Lord. The walkin' word of Jesus Christ.

ELIZABETH *goes to him, looking for trouble.*

Hey! You ready for the parade, Padre?

MARLOWE. The parade?

ELIZABETH. The parade – the parade. All the holy saints. Parading up and down. The nuns showed us at Jesus camp last summer – up at Camp Jesus. They had all the children doin' it. (*Starts to demonstrate.*) Head up and shoulders back, parading up and down – all night long. You go up, up, up, up. Wave and turn round and you go down, up, up, up, up, wave and turn.

MARIANNE *puts a letter on the mantel and goes.*

Then parade over this way and acknowledge the saints. And this way and acknowledge the damned, look at them all there, God help them, and you parade over this way and acknowledge all the babies who died unbaptized. And this way, parading, parading, parading.

As she demonstrates, MARLOWE *goes to her box of dollars under the chair. He takes her money, putting it in his trouser pocket.*

Wait a minute. Now you just wait one goddamn minute.

She goes to him and tries to get her money back.

You give me that.

MARLOWE. Get your hands off me.

They struggle.

Take your hands off me!

ELIZABETH. You give me that!

She has her hand in his trouser pocket, but he fights her off just as MRS NEILSEN *comes in.*

MRS NEILSEN. What are you doing?

MARLOWE. This woman is trying to rob me

ELIZABETH. He took my dollars! You give 'em back.

They go at it again, struggling.

MARLOWE. I will call the police!

MRS NEILSEN *gets between them, she pulls* ELIZABETH *back.*

I'm not gonna stay in this madhouse a moment longer.

ELIZABETH *runs to her box.*

ELIZABETH. Look! Look! He put my dollars in his pocket!

MRS NEILSEN. Where's her dollars?

MARLOWE. I have no idea.

ELIZABETH. They're in his pocket, Aggie.

MARLOWE. Oh, come on!

ELIZABETH (*going to his pocket and pointing*). You can see 'em through the material, look at 'em bulging in his pants.

MARLOWE. I've never been so insulted. Only this woman is so clearly unwell I'd fetch a lawman and have a case. But I am a gentleman and I believe in God's grace. Therefore I'll allow the matter lie and be about my way.

MRS NEILSEN. Did you take her dollars?

MARLOWE. Madam, I am warning you. Do not join this accusation. Good day.

MRS NEILSEN. Did you take her dollars, you panhandling son of a bitch?

MARLOWE (*menacing*). Madam…

MRS NEILSEN. You best give her something from the church.

MARLOWE. I have no church.

MRS NEILSEN. What a shocker. Give her some alms then. Ain't that what the Bible says?

MARLOWE. I am a poor man myself.

MRS NEILSEN. Show me your pockets.

MARLOWE. I beg your pardon?

MRS NEILSEN. Show me your pockets.

MARLOWE. What would that prove?

MRS NEILSEN. Humor me.

Pause. MARLOWE *tries to go.* MRS NEILSEN *stands in his way.*

ELIZABETH. It's on the knicky knacky noo now!

MARLOWE. Why don't you give her some alms? Ha? What you got in those pockets? I know you're coming into money, huh?

He crowds MRS NEILSEN, *walking against her.*

MRS NEILSEN. You stay off a me.

MARLOWE (*quietly*). You wanna get into this? You wanna get into 'What's in your pockets?' What's in *your* pockets, huh?

MARLOWE *pushes* MRS NEILSEN *against the furniture, his hands on her.*

What's in your pockets? What's in *your* pockets?

This is all happening quietly but MARLOWE *is determined and forceful.*

What are you anyway? Whatcha doing? Skulking round the world like a loose chipping. What are you, huh?

He is pressed against her, trapping her, reaching into the pockets of her skirt.

MRS NEILSEN. Let me go.

ELIZABETH *goes to the dresser. She finds a revolver in behind books on an upper shelf. She points it at* MARLOWE.

ELIZABETH. Hey, preacher.

MARLOWE *sees the gun. He cowers.*

MARLOWE. Jesus Christ!

ELIZABETH. That's right.

She shoots, once, twice, three times, four times, five times, emptying the gun, trying to hit MARLOWE, *who dodges away on the far side of the room. Bullets shatter crockery, lamps, pictures hanging on the walls, but somehow, miraculously, he is unharmed. The revolver starts to click, click, click as* ELIZABETH *keeps trying to fire the empty weapon.* MRS NEILSEN *stands frozen, her hands over her ears.*

MARLOWE. Stop it! Stop!

He pulls the dollars from his pocket and throws them on the ground.

ELIZABETH. Thank you! You see? Good manners will always trump a scoundrel.

She retrieves her money as GENE *comes in.*

MARLOWE. This is a fucking madhouse.

ELIZABETH. Then get out, right?

MARLOWE. I'm getting out.

ELIZABETH. Well then go.

MARLOWE. I am.

ELIZABETH. Well go then.

MARLOWE. I'm going.

GENE. Mom.

NICK *comes in, breathless, wet and dirty from being up on the roof in the rain.*

NICK. What the hell is going on? (*To* MRS NEILSEN.) What happened?

MRS NEILSEN. Ask him.

MARLOWE. I have been accused and degraded, sir. Here in this very room.

NICK. We've all been degraded in this very room. Who was shooting?

MRS NEILSEN. It doesn't matter.

MARLOWE (*leaving*). With ye prayers will ye seek ye repentance.

ELIZABETH. That's right.

MARLOWE *stalks out.*

NICK (*to* GENE). See to your mother.

GENE *tries to sort* ELIZABETH *out. She knocks him away with a shout.* MRS NEILSEN *steps in and takes*

ELIZABETH *out gently*. NICK *and* GENE *are alone*.
GENE *is holding his mother's money box*.

GENE. You can't…

NICK. What?

GENE. She's gonna kill someone.

NICK. Mm. Water's pouring in up there. Goddamn pipes have burst. Only hope now is they'll freeze.

GENE. Right. You gonna go down the pier?

NICK. For what?

GENE. Marianne just told me that's where she's going. You have any opinion about that?

NICK (*shrugs*). That guy seems like a…

GENE. Like a what?

NICK (*sniffs and wipes his nose while he tidies up*). He seems strong.

GENE. Well that's alright then. Too bad she didn't feel like saying goodbye I guess.

NICK. Well, that's… [a pity.]

NICK *is looking at some broken crockery*.

GENE. It's what?

NICK. Well that's a pity.

GENE. That's a pity, huh?

NICK. I think so.

GENE. Yeah?

NICK. Yeah.

GENE. You don't give a damn.

NICK. I did my best.

GENE. You did your best.

NICK. What did you want me to do? What would you do? Kick her in the street?

GENE. Well she's in the street now! Why couldn't ya just let her stay here?

NICK. There is no here! I don't own a 'here'! I only ever borrowed it, Gene! You got a job and that's... it's gonna be okay.

GENE. I don't have a job.

NICK. But you had the letter.

GENE. I was too late. Job was gone.

NICK. And you just took that?!

GENE. Well what else could I do?

NICK. You coulda said something... Jesus Christ, you shoulda said something to me! What are you doing? Instead you lied to me about it?

GENE. I didn't want to embarrass you!

NICK. Embarrass *me*?

GENE. 'Cause you were all, 'This guy is my buddy. And she's my old girlfriend and this is all gonna be great.'

NICK. Aw, Gene!! Jesus Christ!

GENE. What are you so worried about? My plans don't work out, they don't work out, what do you care?

NICK. Because I needed you to just do this one thing for me.

GENE. Why? Why is it so important?

NICK. Because I needed you to... I don't have anything to give you.

GENE. Why do you have to give me anything?

NICK. What kinda question is that?

GENE. It's a... what? Don't worry about it.

NICK. Look, me and your mother...

The band gently play underscore, the weeping descending
phrase that opens 'Lay Lady Lay'…

GENE. What…

NICK. We're not gonna be here.

GENE. Where are you going?

NICK. We're going all the way.

GENE. All the way where?

NICK. All the way.

GENE. Dad, don't joke like that.

NICK. It's no joke. Your mother will go first, and…

Pause. GENE *sees that* NICK *is holding the revolver.*

GENE. Don't say this to me, Pa.

NICK. It's alright. It's okay. It would happen some time, right?

GENE. Don't say this to me.

NICK. It's alright! It's like when you were always scared of the
    carousel at the Christmas fair? The lights and the music, it
    was all just too much? No one could understand why you
    were crying and you wanted to get off. All the other kids
    laughing and trying to get on. But I understood it. I know.
    Sometimes you just have to get off. (*Laughs.*) I know!

GENE. This is crazy!

NICK. That's right. It is. It's crazy. I been flailing around, Gene.
    I gotta stop.

    GENE *takes* ELIZABETH, *putting her behind him, standing*
    in front of her protectively.

GENE. Dad. Don't… don't do that. I'll get a job. I'll get one.

NICK. Yeah, get a job. A few dollars ain't gonna get us out of
    this one.

GENE. Give me a chance.

NICK. Whatcha gonna do? Suddenly write a masterpiece all of
    a sudden?

GENE. Maybe. Maybe I will.

ELIZABETH. Just go, Gene.

NICK. I'm sorry, son.

Silence. GENE *doesn't know what to say.*

GENE. Where am I gonna go?

NICK *puts his hand in his pocket.*

NICK. Go wherever you… this is twenty-two dollars… it's everything I got.

GENE *looks at the money.*

I love you, son.

GENE. I'm… gonna go.

NICK. That's right. You do that.

As GENE *goes,* MRS NEILSEN, MRS BURKE, KATE *and* MARIANNE *are singing the second verse and chorus of 'Jokerman'.*

Jokerman

So swiftly the sun sets in the sky
You rise up and say goodbye to no one
Fools rush in where angels fear to tread
Both of their futures, so full of dread, you don't show one
Shedding off one more layer of skin
Keeping one step ahead of the persecutor within

Jokerman dance to the nightingale tune
Bird fly high by the light of the moon
Oh, oh, oh, Jokerman

DR WALKER *addresses us.* ELIZABETH *is playing 'Clair de Lune' on the piano.*

DR WALKER. Last time I saw Nick Laine was the morning of Friday November 30th 1934. Why'd I call by? Christ knows. Just a feeling somewhere. And a strange idea – and maybe it was the truth, and if it was maybe it mighta cheered him up,

I don't know. He seemed good when I saw him. He seemed alright. That's the… That's something I've come to recognize. Once the decision is made. Hardest thing in life, right? Making up your mind?

Daylight. Time has passed. MRS NEILSEN *comes in to find* NICK, MR BURKE *and* MRS BURKE *in the dining room.* MRS BURKE *is making lists.* NICK *is helping her.* DR WALKER *stands with* MR BURKE *near the window.* MRS NEILSEN *is in her best clothes, a jacket, and a hat.* THE BURKES *are both wearing formal mourning attire.* ELIZABETH *also stands in the room*

MRS NEILSEN. I'm sorry. I don't want to intrude. There's a taxi outside.

MR BURKE. Not at all! Mrs Neilsen.

DR WALKER *nods a hello to* MRS NEILSEN.

MRS BURKE. Oh, Mrs Neilsen, we are going to miss you, you know.

MRS NEILSEN. I will miss you. I'm only sorry I won't be able to be with you for the ceremony.

MRS BURKE. We could never ask you to come all the way up north with us! We'd never expect it.

MRS NEILSEN. Is there anything I can do?

MRS BURKE. Oh no. When we get home it's … it's only going to be small – of necessity – but we'll… it's a pretty cemetery, Mrs Neilsen, it's… (*Fights back tears.*) Good and evil – it's all beyond them, isn't it?

MRS NEILSEN. Oh, entirely.

MR BURKE. Well we better… They said to us, you know, that slipway is notorious where he… You turn round, someone is gone, and the current just…

DR WALKER. It's not the first time.

MRS BURKE. They really need to…

MR BURKE. It's crazy!

MRS NEILSEN. Yes, it's terrible.

MR BURKE. You've been a good friend to us, Mrs Neilsen. You make sure and write. We should stay in touch.

MRS NEILSEN. Absolutely.

MRS BURKE *kisses* MRS NEILSEN. MR BURKE *shakes her hand.*

Let me walk you out.

MRS BURKE. Thank you, Mrs Neilsen.

MR BURKE. George.

They shake hands.

Nick.

DR WALKER *is alone with* NICK *and* ELIZABETH.

NICK. You okay, Doc? You want some coffee?

DR WALKER. No, I better go.

DR WALKER *pauses at the door.*

I've always admired you, Nick.

MRS NEILSEN *comes in.*

NICK. Are you fucking crazy?

DR WALKER. No, I… You just keep on that road, alright? (*Goes.*)

NICK (*to* MRS NEILSEN). What time is your bus?

MRS NEILSEN. Eleven.

NICK. You want something to eat?

MRS NEILSEN *shakes her head.*

MRS NEILSEN. How did it go? Down at the bank this morning?

NICK. Oh, the bank! They got some new guy in charge of the loans. New hotshot. Looks fifteen years old. Talked some crazy talk. Says there's a tide coming is gonna lift all boats. Says let's keep talking. Talk again in the New Year.

MRS NEILSEN. Well that's great.

NICK. You look very pretty.

MRS NEILSEN. I got a child inside me, Nick.

NICK. What? How did that happen?

MRS NEILSEN. The way it usually happens.

NICK. I thought you was too old.

MRS NEILSEN. Why thank you. I guess not.

NICK. Well, Jesus Christ, this is… this is… you can't go now.

MRS NEILSEN. Why not?

MRS NEILSEN *comes to him. Too much to be said. Can't be said.*

Goodbye, Elizabeth.

ELIZABETH. You're too good for him, Mrs Neilsen.

MRS NEILSEN *smiles. She silently goes out.* NICK *stands there.*

What was that crock of shit you just told her?

NICK. She don't need to know.

He goes to the dresser, takes out the revolver and loads it.

ELIZABETH. What they really say?

NICK. We gotta get out. We gotta be out by the third of next month.

ELIZABETH. When is that?

NICK. Monday. You wanna do that? Go walkin' the roads? Sleepin' in a ditch?

ELIZABETH. Not really! Well, mister. You done it. You got 'em all out. I don't know how. But you did it.

She comes to him and takes the revolver. She looks at it.

I know. You start off – it's a love story. You wait outside the drug store where you said you'd meet her, searchin' in the eyes of everyone passing by. You can't believe it when she steps out of the crowd. Her face, perhaps plain to everybody else, well it uncloaks its beauty just for you. And you know you're gone. You're her hostage. And she takes you down into a world of plans and dreams you could never have sustained on your own.

And then one day in the midst of the exhilaration and the worry and the children and the fighting and the whole damn shebang, one day you realize you're just about scraping through. And you look up and you see her again and you may as well be looking at a baby giraffe in the zoo.

She's alive and she sees you but her world is not your world. You don't want to live in her world and she doesn't want you there anyhow. But you know you're too weak on your own. The children look to you. 'What are you looking at me for?' you say. And they hate you and you're glad they hate you. 'Cause they stop coming to you.

And then one day she turns round and says, 'I don't love you any more either,' and you think, 'What the hell does that have to do with anything?!' Except you know she's just knocked you out cold. And you realize, 'Oh shit, I'm really on my own here now. Okay, okay, that's alright. I can drink myself to death in some room somewhere – it's alright.'

She opens the revolver.

Until she loses her mind. And then you have her for ever.

She empties the bullets on to the floor.

You have her for ever. So what do you say we live a little longer?

ELIZABETH *sings.*

Forever Young

>May God bless and keep you always
>May your wishes all come true
>May you always do for others
>And let others do for you

> May you build a ladder to the stars
> And climb on every rung
> May you stay forever young
> Forever young, forever young
> May you stay forever young
>
> May you grow up to be righteous
> May you grow up to be true
> May you always know the truth
> And see the lights surrounding you
> May you always be courageous
> Stand upright and be strong
> May you stay forever young

The cast join her, quietly at first, perhaps building to an unexpected strength.

> Forever young, forever young
> May you stay forever young

DR WALKER *is before us.*

DR WALKER. Word was Nick headed south, took Elizabeth with him, took care of her best he could. Made it down as far at Sioux City till bronchitis got her in a flophouse down there. They took her into a home for women on the banks of the Missouri. Nick stayed nearby in a hostel for men. Came down to see her every day. He was with her the morning she passed. Held her hand at the end, I heard. I don't know where he went after that. Word was he kept on heading south, maybe down towards Oklahoma, but nobody really knew.

We see NICK *and* ELIZABETH *having dinner – happy and healthy.* GENE *joins them.*

Old Mr Perry gave Gene a place to stay, a job and working in his store. He tried his hand at reporting for a local paper then took the plunge and went down to New York City. He met a girl there, it didn't work out. When the war came he enlisted in the Marines, saw action in Italy and then at Okinawa where he stood on a mine and was declared missing in action June of '45.

MARIANNE *comes and sits. The family are happy together.*

I left this world eleven years earlier, on Christmas Eve 1934. Set it all up. It was just like stepping through a glass wall. I could still see everything. Saw the time come and go. Saw Marianne and her Joseph come by the following winter. And damn if she didn't have a baby in her arms! Yes, she had a baby. They were well dressed in warm coats. Came up and stood outside the old inn with that baby in their arms. They looked up at the windows a while, then I watched them walk away.

I looked out on the water. Then I closed my eyes.

End.

Acknowledgements

All words and music by Bob Dylan, unless otherwise indicated.

'Sign On The Window'
Copyright © 1970 by Big Sky Music; renewed 1998 by Big Sky Music. All rights reserved. International copyright secured. Reprinted by permission.

'Went To See The Gypsy'
Copyright © 1970 by Big Sky Music; renewed 1998 by Big Sky Music. All rights reserved. International copyright secured. Reprinted by permission.

'Tight Connection To My Heart (Has Anyone Seen My Love)'
Copyright © 1985 by Special Rider Music. All rights reserved. International copyright secured. Reprinted by permission.

'Slow Train'
Copyright © 1979 by Special Rider Music. All rights reserved. International copyright secured. Reprinted by permission.

'License To Kill'
Copyright © 1983 by Special Rider Music. All rights reserved. International copyright secured. Reprinted by permission.

'I Want You'
Copyright © 1966 by Dwarf Music; renewed 1994 by Dwarf Music. All rights reserved. International copyright secured. Reprinted by permission.

'Like A Rolling Stone'
Copyright © 1965 by Warner Bros. Inc.; renewed 1993 by Special Rider Music. All rights reserved. International copyright secured. Reprinted by permission.

'You Ain't Goin' Nowhere'
Copyright © 1967 by Dwarf Music; renewed 1995 by Dwarf Music. All rights reserved. International copyright secured. Reprinted by permission.

'Jokerman'
Copyright © 1983 by Special Rider Music. All rights reserved. International copyright secured. Reprinted by permission.

'Sweetheart Like You'
Copyright © 1983 by Special Rider Music. All rights reserved. International copyright secured. Reprinted by permission.

'True Love Tends To Forget'
Copyright © 1978 by Special Rider Music. All rights reserved. International copyright secured. Reprinted by permission.

'Hurricane'
Written by Bob Dylan with Jacques Levy. Copyright © 1975 by Ram's Horn Music; renewed 2003 by Ram's Horn Music. All rights reserved. International copyright secured. Reprinted by permission.